A People's History of the German Revolution

People's History

History tends to be viewed from the perspective of the rich and powerful, where the actions of small numbers are seen to dictate the course of world affairs. But this perspective conceals the role of ordinary women and men, as individuals or as parts of collective organisations, in shaping the course of history. The People's History series puts ordinary people and mass movements centre stage and looks at the great moments of the past from the bottom up.

The People's History series was founded and edited by William A. Pelz (1951–2017).

Also available:

Long Road to Harpers Ferry
The Rise of the First American Left
Mark A. Lause

A People's History of the Portuguese Revolution
Raquel Varela

A People's History of the German Revolution

1918–19

William A. Pelz

Foreword by Mario Kessler

First published 2018 by Pluto Press
345 Archway Road, London N6 5AA

www.plutobooks.com

Copyright © the Estate of William A. Pelz 2018

British Library Cataloguing in Publication Data
A catalogue record for this book is available from the British Library

ISBN   978 0 7453 3711 1   Hardback
ISBN   978 0 7453 3710 4   Paperback
ISBN   978 1 7868 0248 4   PDF eBook
ISBN   978 1 7868 0250 7   Kindle eBook
ISBN   978 1 7868 0249 1   EPUB eBook

This book is printed on paper suitable for recycling and made from fully managed
and sustained forest sources. Logging, pulping and manufacturing processes are
expected to conform to the environmental standards of the country of origin.

Typeset by Stanford DTP Services, Northampton, England

Simultaneously printed in the United Kingdom and United States of America

Contents

Foreword

Mario Kessler

A People's History of the German Revolution, 1918–19, is the last book by the American historian William Arthur ("Bill") Pelz, who died at age 66 on December 10, 2017 in his hometown of Chicago.

The son of a bus driver, Bill Pelz was connected to working people by origin and attitude. He wrote his doctoral thesis in 1988, inspired by Arthur Rosenberg's classic work *The Birth of the German Republic*, on the Spartacus League in the German November Revolution.* Documentary books on Eugene V. Debs and Wilhelm Liebknecht followed. *Against Capitalism: The European Left on the March* was published in 2008, *Karl Marx: A World to Win* four years later, *German Social Democracy: A Documentary History* in 2015, and finally *A People's History of Modern Europe* in 2016. Among his numerous editorial works, his contributions to the *Encyclopedia of the European Left* and his appointment as a co-editor of Rosa Luxemburg's works in English must also be mentioned. A lifelong Chicagoan, he held positions as a contingent professor at Roosevelt University, and then as Director of Social Science Programs at De Paul University. For the past 20 years, the Marxist historian was professor of European history and political science at Elgin Community College on the outskirts of Chicago.

A People's History of the German Revolution, 1918–19, a manuscript completed by Pelz just days before his unexpected loss, returns the author to the starting point of his career as a historian.

---

* Arthur Rosenberg's book *Die Entstehung der deutschen Republik* was first published in 1928. An English translation by Ian F. D. Morrow followed in 1931. It was reprinted in several issues.

The title should remind us of Howard Zinn's *A People's History of the United States*. Both Zinn's and Pelz's works unashamedly make the social history of working-class women and men accessible, vital and popular. Yet, unlike Zinn's documentary approach, Pelz's interpretive history of the German Revolution might benefit from an introduction to the historical context of this crucial moment in German and working-class history for those less familiar with German history. Why should readers be curious about this book, a brilliant and entirely fresh overview of an important period of German and European history?

The book introduces the reader to German social history of the nineteenth and early-twentieth centuries; a time that seems distant, but whose problems, as this book shows, remain present today. Compared to England and France, Germany was a belated nation: its bourgeoisie only appeared as a historical force when it felt the breath of the emerging working class at its neck. Thus, in the European revolutionary year of 1848, the middle class was neither willing nor able to fight out the struggle for national unity together with lower classes, especially workers. Instead, the German bourgeoisie allied itself with the forces led by Prussian Chancellor Otto von Bismarck. After the Prussians fought and won three wars against their neighbors, they unified the new state "from above"; in 1871, most German-speaking territories became part of a new German Empire (with the notable exception of Austria which remained part of the Habsburg Empire). This sealed the alliance between the emerging imperialist bourgeoisie and the old nobility, the class which provided the German military and diplomatic elite.

Denied any meaningful political role in the new state, workers were attracted to the Social Democratic Party (SPD), whose path to the strongest electoral force in the German Empire is impressively traced in this book. The social-democratic workers and the left-wing intellectuals supporting them formed an increasingly dense network of trade unions, media, cooperatives and cultural organizations whose structures grew as an alternative to the dominant culture of bourgeois German society.

But this social-democratic counter-society faced a dilemma: the more it grew into a counter-society in the state, the more its leaders and administrative functionaries no longer wanted to eliminate this state. Rather than "abolish" bourgeois society in the Hegelian sense, SPD leaders and theorists sought to peacefully take over the states' institutions through social and electoral reform. At the same time, revolutionary rhetoric remained central to SPD theory.

As early as 1896, Bertrand Russell* sharply recognized that this contradiction within the SPD overlapped the fundamental contradiction of German society—that the largest and strongest class remained excluded from participation in society. Although men, but not women, had universal, equal and secret suffrage in the Reich, the German parliament, the *Reichstag*, had no real executive power in comparison with the Emperor. In Prussia, by far the most important of the German states, a three-class franchise system gave the dispossessed classes less voting rights than the upper class. Moreover, the SPD's increasing bureaucratic direction resulted in a distinct cultural cleavage between the party's career-oriented professionalism and its working-class electoral and trade union base.

Social Democratic Party leaders believed that through an alliance with the liberal wing of the bourgeoisie they would gain one concession after another from the ruling classes, resulting in the conditions for a peaceful transition to socialism. A minority in the party criticized these policies as reformist illusions, Rosa Luxemburg perhaps most notably. The Polish Marxist, who devoted her life to the German workers' movement, came to understand most precisely that the liberal bourgeoisie would rather seek a compromise with the reactionary landlords, industrialists, and the military at the expense of the working class, and that the

---

* Bertrand Russell, *German Social Democracy: Six Lectures* (Longmans, Green, and Company, 1896).

ruling elites would never give away class power to workers in the form of civil and economic rights. In fact, the Imperial Court, the landlords and the military forged an ever stronger alliance with the industrial and financial capital in order to realize their great political project, that Germany would be elevated from the rank of a European power to the rank of the pre-eminent European power, and a world power, even if it required deadly war with neighboring states.

The war that began in August 1914 was in fact a consequence of the imperialist policies of Germany as well as its allies and opponents, and waged by all warring parties with great brutality and without consideration for human losses. In the first industrialized war, all available human and material resources were mobilized to sustain the war effort. Bill Pelz's book examines evidence and reports from frontline soldiers, and workers' and soldiers' wives and families, to depict conditions and acts of resistance at the front and in the hinterland. The increasing number of strikes and intensifying labor conflict in war-time Germany—revolutionary preludes—are of particular interest. Here the book incisively demonstrates how much the common people, and especially women, are a force of history. Pelz also shows the ways in which the unique contributions of intellectuals, working-class activists, and women and men from right to left, from Victor Klemperer to Käte and Hermann Duncker, actively and consciously sought to influence German politics and society.

At the end of the war both losers and victors found themselves in a state of utter exhaustion. Everywhere economies were in disarray. In Tsarist Russia, Austria-Hungary, and Imperial Germany governmental systems collapsed entirely. Even before the armistice had been signed, a rebellion against Imperial German authorities by soldiers and workers seeking an end to the slaughter and the starvation, initiated the German Revolution of 1918–19.

As a consequence of the military defeat of Germany and the anger of the masses, and triggered by a naval mutiny, in days the revolution spread throughout the whole country. There was no appreciable resistance from the old order. Workers joined forces with sailors and soldiers in an enormous mass movement against the monarchical system. Throughout Germany workers' and soldiers' councils mushroomed, instantly and organically assuming political power. Social Democracy found itself at the head of the revolution, but it was, since 1917, split into a Majority Social Democratic Party (MSPD) encompassing the old reformist politics, and an Independent Social Democratic Party of Germany (USPD) with support from the Spartacus League at its left wing. Most of the councils identified with the MSPD, but the moment was complicated as the base of the mass movement, and some of its leaders, came to be equally influenced by the radical left.

On November 9, 1918, Emperor William II abdicated. Friedrich Ebert, chair of the MSPD, became Chancellor of Germany, and another MSPD leader, Philipp Scheidemann, proclaimed the new republic. A few hours later, Karl Liebknecht of the Spartacus League proclaimed the "Free Socialist Republic". These competing proclamations reflected the conflict that underlay the revolution. While the MSPD called for a Constituent National Assembly to be convened without delay, the USPD and the Spartacus League advocated the rapid realization of Socialist ideals based on the existing system of workers' and soldiers' councils.

That same day, a nationwide "Council of People's Representatives" was formed to ratify a new provisional government of the General Assembly of the Berlin Workers' and Soldiers' Councils. The six-member Council comprised three MSPD and three USPD representatives, co-chaired by Friedrich Ebert (MSPD) and Hugo Haase (USPD). A key role in the revolution devolved to Ebert in his dual role as Chancellor of Germany and parliamentary leader and co-chair of this Council of People's Representatives: a temporary government reflecting the demands of the workers' councils from below and the traditional SPD institutions of the established pro-war leadership. Ebert also secretly secured the support of the military for this precarious government. The Council of People's Representatives legislated votes for women

(November 12), then declared that elections to a constituent National Assembly would be held on January 19, 1919.

At the end of 1918 Germany faced a situation of dual power. On the one hand, the Council of People's Representatives exercised formal legal and executive power. On the other hand, the revolution had swept from power large parts of the old regime. For a few weeks at least, workers', soldiers' and sailors' councils constituted the real power base.

The text critically examines the MSPD dilemma as a set of challenges which inherently limited the MSPD's response and political maneuverability. The lost war, the repatriation of several million troops and the provision of food supplies, and the fear of bringing the country to the brink of civil war, left the MSPD no choice but to cooperate with the reactionary civic and military administrative bodies of Imperial Germany.

Crucially, however, Pelz cites evidence that fundamentally reshapes this interpretation. The book shows that the MSPD leaders primarily wanted first to maintain their administrative and governmental positions. Thus, they required the support of the old Imperial institutions of military, nobility, and industry. Second, they explicitly feared radicalism from below, feared the overthrow of capitalism, and actively and creatively worked to stem the tide of rebellion. On the eve of the Emperor's abdication, MSPD leader and future first German President Ebert complained that "if the Emperor does not abdicate the social revolution is unavoidable. But I don't want it; indeed I hate it like sin."*

Using the prestige of the MSPD, still supported by many German workers as "their" party, its leaders sought to stabilize capitalist social relations. MSPD tactics included forming councils under their control. Further, when the Revolution brought demands for socialization—nationalization under democratic control—the Council of People's Representatives decided in mid-November

---

* Friedrich Ebert, as quoted in: Heinrich August Winkler, *Germany: The Long Road West*, translated by Alexander J. Sager, Vol. I: *1789–1933* (Oxford and New York: Oxford University Press, 2006), p. 331.

to establish a committee that would decide which industries were "ripe" for socialization, then adjourned the committee with no substantial recommendations. When the first National Congress of Workers' and Soldiers' Councils opened on December 16, 1918, Ebert declared that "the victorious proletariat will not institute class rule."*

By the end of 1918, MSPD leaders had begun to deploy far right military troops, the *Freikorps* (Free Corps), near Berlin to prepare to defeat the Revolution.

The People's Naval Division, a force that originally had been sent to Berlin to safeguard the MSPD but which had become increasingly radicalized, was attacked on December 24. The division had participated in a Spartacist-led demonstration and held MSPD leader Otto Wels hostage, prompting the Ebert-led government to order its main forces discharged. When the sailors refused, the SPD sent other military units, resulting in the Bloody Christmas events in which sailors successfully defended themselves.

On December 29, 1918, the alliance between the MSPD and the USPD in the provisional government collapsed when the USPD withdrew from the Council of People's Representatives. Days later the revolutionary conflict escalated into the so-called Spartacus Revolt of January 1919: troops sent by the MSPD government, and assisted by *Freikorps*, bloodily suppressed this uprising. This was a welcome pretext for *Freikorps* units to attack the communists. On January 15, 1919, *Freikorps* troops killed Rosa Luxemburg and Karl Liebknecht. Both had founded the Communist Party of Germany (KPD) on New Year's Day 1919 with part of the Spartacus League and other radicals.

The murder of Luxemburg and Liebknecht, and other revolutionary leaders, was a major blow against the Revolution and the KPD in particular, but it was not the end of revolutionary struggles

* Friedrich Ebert, *Schriften, Aufzeichnungen, Reden*, Vol. II (Dresden: Carl Reissner Verlag, 1926), p. 139.

that continued in Bremen, the Ruhr region, Bavaria and other parts of Germany. Nevertheless, the elections to the National Assembly on January 19, 1919, turned the path decisively towards the new bourgeois order. The MSPD emerged from the elections as the strongest party. On February 6, the National Assembly constituted itself in Weimar and on February 11 Friedrich Ebert became first President of the new German republic. The government was composed of MSPD, Center Party and German Democratic Party, with Philipp Scheidemann as Chancellor (Prime Minister). Most of the workers' and soldiers' councils had dissolved themselves by the summer of 1919. Others were violently disbanded. Even when defeated in 1918–19, however, the movement remained strong enough to prevent right-wing counter-revolutionaries from crushing all democratic rights and progressive social reforms. The counter-revolution was still forced to take a democratic form, often dressing itself in socialist disguise.

The Emperor left, but the generals remained.* Political elites and big business retained their power. Despite a democratic Weimar constitution and the achievement of women's suffrage, elites wedded to the old order would seek to destroy the first German Republic and continued to dream of Germany's bid for European and world dominance. The unfinished Revolution of 1918–19 resulted only in a precarious democracy, which was usurped by full-fledged counterrevolution in 1933 when the Nazis took power.

Like the historian Arthur Rosenberg, Pelz shows the ways in which the workers' and soldiers' councils became the real possibility for the establishment of a revolutionary-democratic order, one that could eliminate the old class rule, and establish real social and civil liberties. In so doing, the book restores the revolutionary potential of the period's history. And here also lies

---

* *The Kaiser Goes, the Generals Remain* (*Der Kaiser ging, die Generäle blieben*) was the title of Theodor Plievier's 1932 anti-war novel that was translated, in 1933, into English.

the particular strength of the book—giving voice to ordinary men and women in uniform and at home. Pelz accurately and expertly gives us these ordinary women and men in their due place, as the most important, and conscious, historical actors of their time and place.

Professor Dr. Mario Kessler
Center for Contemporary History
Potsdam, Germany

Introduction:
What German Revolution?

We are all prisoners. Captives of our place in time and space; bound by our own history. As has been said, the past is another country—distant, strange and seemingly unknowable. To understand this odd and faraway land, we must use our imagination. For the following pages to make any sense at all, one must try to imagine a world before the internet, Facebook, Google, mobile phones or jet planes. And, also a world before the horrors of fascism, nuclear arms, murderous drones, seemingly endless bloodshed in the Near East or climate change. We must not think of the past as it was portrayed by the famous *Flintstones* cartoons of the twentieth century. That is, a past in which people were just like us albeit with funny clothing. This bias of present-mindedness is subtle and hard to overcome. It is just one of the pitfalls we must overcome to reach a fairer approximation of actual history.

While scholars must always avoid made up facts or "fake history,"[1] the notion of simply "getting the facts right" is not quite so easy. Despite clichés to the contrary, facts never speak for themselves. Rather, historians, writers, and speakers must study and interpret these facts to give them context and validity. People often say, "just give me the straight facts" or that they only want to learn objective history. The problem with this, as E. H. Carr noted, is that the "facts of history cannot be purely objective, since they become facts of history only in virtue of the significance attached to them by the historian."[2] Not only must historians con-textualize and interpret facts, they must select which facts they will use. This process results in what is called the bias of selection. Each page an author devotes to one topic or perspective may well be at the cost of overlooking other events or perspectives. Each minute a teacher talks of one thing she must neglect another.

Another problem historians face is that the thoughts, hopes and fears of average women and men often are interned with their bones. In other words, they die without leaving any written record behind. It is different with the upper heights of society. While a Krupp[3] may leave rooms full of documents and correspondence, a Krause[4] often leaves behind only a handful of trinkets that may not readily speak to their lives. This bias of survival means historians struggle to find the historical footprint of common people who normally leave neither massive archives nor long published biographies.

Unfortunately, most scholars are all too human, and subject to all the emotions, prejudices and ideological assumptions that plague their species. So, some historians unwittingly fall into confirmation bias. This means they search and interpret evidence to fit within a preconceived set of beliefs. Let us take the case of Winston Churchill, a well-known British politician and later prime minister. He commented extensively on the revolutions that rocked Europe in the latter part of World War I. While he did acknowledge material or economic factors on several occasions, Churchill had a habit of returning to a conspiratorial view of history.

Talking of "schemes of the International Jews," the future World War II leader contended that from the

days of Spartacus-Weishaupt[5] to those of Karl Marx, and down to Trotsky (Russia), Bela Kun (Hungary), Rosa Luxembourg (Germany), and Emma Goldman (United States), this world-wide conspiracy for the overthrow of civilisation and for the reconstitution of society on the basis of arrested development, of envious malevolence, and impossible equality, has been steadily growing.[6]

He also blamed Jews for "the tragedy of the French Revolution" as well as for "every subversive movement during the Nineteenth Century."[7] Although anti-Semitism may be the first odor one smells, it is likewise apparent that Churchill's worldview was simple and dualistic; he saw some people as good (Churchill and his ilk), some as bad (International Jews and radicals).

Still, one should understand that these ideological biases were not strictly personal, rather they reflected the biases of the contemporary culture and nation-state more broadly. After all, people learn to have certain prejudices and to look at the world in a particular manner; they are rarely capricious or random. It was not threatening to but reinforcing of the British Empire to have Churchill and others to blame a conspiracy of "International Jews" for revolutions. These revolutions could just as easily be seen as popular reaction to injustice and exploitation. Ruling classes spend a lot of energy, both consciously and unconsciously, to promote a sympathetic historical narrative.

Why else build all those monuments and museums? Why create universities or support unemployed intellectuals?[8] The rulers and the rich do such things because they seek legitimacy. "All rulers needed an interpretation of the past to justify the authority of their government," one scholar noted, "The past has always been the handmaid of authority."[9] Compare and contrast, for example, the government-supported German History Museum in central Berlin in 1988 versus 2018. In 1988, the museum was oriented toward the political line of East Germany's ruling party. That meant Martin Luther was bad and peasant revolts were good. Thirty years later it is, in essence, the other way around.

Remember history is more than a parade of famous men, with the occasional token woman thrown in for diversity. The idea that only a few individuals make history has a long and deep pedigree and is only overcome with difficulty. One much admired British historian, who some say should have known better, said the "history of modern Europe can be written in terms of three titans: Napoleon, Bismarck, and Lenin."[10] If needed, and space allowed, this example could be amplified by hundreds of comparable pronouncements. At least in many survey courses in the English-speaking world, German history starts with Otto von Bismarck (unification) and goes through Kaiser Wilhelm II (evil militarist), and then pauses to dwell on the unique evil of Hitler.

What the rulers decided and what the great and the good did or thought is, of course, one factor in shaping history. But an often forgotten and vital force is what the common people did or did not do. A case in point: even the greatest Imperial German Admirals found themselves helpless when, in 1918, the sailors of the High Seas Fleet would no longer follow their orders. But, this is not part of the historical narrative that is put forth in school.

Some have denied that there even was a German Revolution in 1918. Textbooks often speak of German defeat in World War I and the establishment of the Weimar Republic with hardly a comment on the upheavals that ended Imperial Germany. In this version of history, US President Woodrow Wilson and his 14 points deserve inclusion in the narrative while the actions of millions of ordinary Germans do not. This narrative is exaggerated and even cartoonish, but more problematic is that it treats the common people of Germany as an inert lump with as much agency or initiative as a common building brick.

For much of the latter part of the twentieth century, many knew nothing about what can be termed the German Revolution. A story from the 1970s, related by the late Robert F. Wheeler illustrates this problem: "A German Revolution after World War I? A West German undergraduate in my German history survey indicated she had never heard of such a thing. And until the early 1960s the same was probably true of most Western academics."[1] For decades the Revolution was either ignored or mentioned only in passing by many historians. This trend was particularly pronounced in the Federal Republic of Germany, which had experienced the events itself. One historian reasons that this was because of the "anti-democratic views of history which Germany's nationalist middle classes had largely accepted before 1933 and which, even after 1945, were only slowly and gradually abandoned."[12]

To give an anecdotal example, the current author recently asked an upper-level class on Modern European History a question. The students were predominately history majors or minors, many of whom plan to teach history in high school or college. When these people were asked, "What was the German Revolution?" their responses were telling. Several thought it was when Hitler burned the Reichstag and seized power. Many others believed it was a reference to the 1989 fall of the Berlin Wall. One guessed it was something to do with Luther and the Reformation. None connected it to a movement that saw millions of people rising up to end World War I, abolish the monarchy and establish a republic.

Of course, there have also been writers who do acknowledge the German Revolution. It was part of the official historical narrative of Soviet Bloc scholars,[13] and East Germany even staked part of its legitimacy on being the inheritors of the revolution. Outside the orbit of Moscow-influenced scholars, other radicals pointed to Germany as proof that revolution was possible in economically advanced societies.[14] Many Marxists have stressed the huge international significance that a successful revolution in Germany would have had.

As problematic as it is that many textbooks omit discussion of the German Revolution, there are stumbling blocks as well with the ways in which many historians who do acknowledge it have assessed it. It is often noted that Lenin said in 1918, "Without Germany, we are lost." This and the related argument that Germany, unlike backward Russia, was a most developed capitalist economy objectively suitable for a socialist transformation are certainly reasonable. It is also rational to speculate that a successful German Revolution may have inspired revolts throughout, at very least, Europe.

The problem with this approach is that it is traditionally wedded to a rather mechanistic theory of the Social Democrats betraying the revolution. The complexities of the revolution within the context of German historical development get lost within a framework that assumes whatever worked in Russia would have worked in Germany. That is, the revolution is presented by some leftists as easily betrayed because radicals hadn't studied enough Russian history. That is, often the historical analysis by the left, which presents the social democrats as the reason for the revolution's failure, misses the mark because it doesn't acknowledge that revolutionary action is complex and one can't expect Russian methods to work equally as well in Germany.

Specifically, the German left is faulted for not having built a "Leninist" vanguard party. After admitting the existence of objective differences between Russia and Germany, the argument is presented that the revolution failed because, in one author's words, what "was lacking was the sort of party that Lenin had been able to build over the previous 20 years."[15] Of course across the planet in the past hundred years, there were copious examples of "Leninist" parties—Moscow-oriented, Trotskyist and other— that failed to lead revolutions. This is not to say that certain Social Democrats didn't betray the revolution, nor that a vanguard party might have been useful for the far left. But neither argument is sufficient to explain events.

This author will repudiate these three common notions about the 1918–19 revolution: (1) that it was less a revolution and more of a collapse; (2) that this period was mere chaos before the normal progression of Germany into a republic, guided by Woodrow Wilson and the Western allies; and (3) that revolutionary failure was solely caused by Social Democracy and the lack of a vanguard party.

Neither should the revolution be seen only as a failure since "as a result of the revolution, Germans lived from 1918 to 1933 in a political order more democratic than anything seen in Germany's past."[16] That this democratic order was destroyed by big business and the army high command, who supported and then handed over power to the Nazis, is subject for another book. Rather than seeing agency as exclusively in the hands of

the victorious powers, the German elites, or even brilliant revolutionaries, this book will contend that it was the actions of the
common people that largely shaped the revolution and the birth
of the Weimar Republic. Imperial Germany was dead by the end
of 1918. There should be no doubt whatsoever about that. The
death certificate was made out by the German people and signed
by the field marshals and generals. The people's elected Reichstag
representatives conducted the funeral. All the while, many of the
common people of Germany cheered till they were as red in their
faces as many were in their politics. Old Imperial Germany was as
dead as the proverbial doornail. It had neither been murdered by
evil conspirators nor was this fatality the product of an accident.
Rather, it was the result of the common people storming onto the
stage of history.

I

Industrialization and the Emergence of the German Working Class

For centuries, "Germany" was little more than a vague geographical expression for any number of distinct, and often mutually hostile, petty states in central Europe. These countries may have all spoken one variations of German but were typically satellites orbiting around greater empires. To the west, German territories, like the Rhineland, looked to France and incorporated aspects of the greater nation's culture from everyday expressions to wine. The city of Hamburg was a trading partner of Great Britain and so looked to the north for both commerce and culture. Bavaria shared her Catholic faith and much of her foreign policy with the Austrian Empire while the Northeastern kingdom of Prussia had a King who was the vassal of the Russian Czar.

Well into the nineteenth century, most of these people identified with whichever regional entity they were born to; they thought of themselves as Saxons, Hessians, Bavarians, or Prussians rather than as Germans. As mentioned above, the German language varied greatly in practice, the basic root language was everywhere modified, often with a bewildering assortment of local slang and manifold pronunciation. Even in the twenty-first century, one may purchase Austrian-German phrasebooks that, if sold largely in jest, fittingly show how variant "German" can be.

In 1871, a German nation-state was created with the unification of German-speaking lands, though this still excluded Austria and German portions of Switzerland. Historians often credit Prussian leader Otto von Bismarck for cleverly engineering this unification; but this was only possible as a result of a series of historical developments. A growing class of capitalists clamored for the economic advantages unification would bring. As Capitalism emerged in numerous German states, it transformed masses of urban plebeians and erstwhile peasants into a class that could only survive by selling its labor power, that is, a working class. At the same time, the structures and institutions left from feudalism most notably the guild system—rotted, later to be swept away forever. While freed from the old feudal fetters, the common people also lost many protections they had grown to depend on: extensive church charity, freedom to collect wood from the common lands, guilds that ensured that at least some artisans could make a good living.

This transformation was uneven and occurred within specific historical confines. Germany, unlike England or France, lacked the experience of a unified feudal nation-state. The division of the German populace into many petty and not so petty principalities meant that the rising middle class or bourgeoisie, as the French would say, struggled for both national unity and the overthrow of feudal productive relationships. This was a mighty task, which the good burghers proved totally incapable of achieving. Their failure left more room for common people lower in the social hierarchy while paradoxically giving the old feudal lords a chance to reinvent themselves as nationalists.

In 1830, the German bourgeoisie led the masses in an attempt to forge a nation-state that would serve their material interests. Unlike their French and English counterparts, the capitalists of Germany were still living in societies abounding in feudal privileges, rights and restrictions. The German bourgeoisie was relatively poor and dispersed by the standards of their neighbors to the West—a situation that put would-be revolutionaries at a distinct disadvantage. Moreover, the separation of the nation into numerous states combined with an unfortunate geographic position, which limited opportunities for Atlantic trade, left the bourgeoisie unable to establish industrial and commercial centers comparable to Lyons, Paris, Manchester or London.

Thus, even though the economic growth of Germany proceeded almost without interruption after 1815, the middle class suffered from its inability to conquer the political supremacy so necessary for its expansion. Of course, the governments of Germany were aware of the contribution the capitalists made to their kingdoms and therefore granted some reforms like the Prussian Tariff of 1818. In fact, a pattern emerged during the struggle between feudal lord and capitalist, which the radical Frederick Engels concisely summed up: "Every political defeat of the middle class drew after it a victory on the field of commercial legislation."[1] Though common people often lived through the same social change and economic growth, they shared unequally in the rewards.

This situation continued from 1830 to 1848, by which time capitalism had grown to sufficient strength that it could no longer sit idly and watch its most important interests hampered by all manner of feudal fetters. At the same time, the common people compared their lot unfavorably with that of the French and of the British. As is so often, the spark that ignited the situation came from abroad. On February 24, 1848, the Parisian masses drove King Louis Philippe out of town, abolished the monarchy and proclaimed a republic.

Within a few weeks, on March 13, Vienna erupted as well, breaking the power of their old regime. This event was quickly imitated in Berlin where an uprising broke out on March 18. In the capitals of the smaller German states similar revolts took place. Although details varied from place to place, the middle-class parties in all the states argued for national unity, constitutional rule and other reforms of a democratic nature. In each German state these revolts were suppressed and the revolution was finally crushed by the end of 1849.

The role of the common people in the drama of 1848–9 remains a matter of great controversy. This results in part from a lack of reliable sources from that time period. In fact, the lack of clear indications of the thoughts and feelings of common people who did not leave the numerous written records of the elites plagues those who seek to write people's history. In any event, the debacle of 1848–9 postponed the unification of Germany and thus allowed the continuation of regionalism.

With the ultimate unification of Germany at the end of the Franco-Prussian War up until the outbreak of World War I, a politically unified nation-state quickly transformed itself into a major industrial power. This rapid technological change created a large and increasingly restless working class. That this new class was created in less than half a century, as opposed to the much longer transition in Great Britain, meant that German society became more polarized than other nations.

To explore these developments, a discussion is needed about the objective conditions of German labor in terms of living standards, lifestyle and so on. This assessment of objective conditions will be balanced through consideration of subjective narratives, that is, voices of workers who lived in that historical period. This examination will not limit itself to the stereotypical male industrial worker. Rather, it will survey male and female and all those workers who lived from labor rather than property, regardless of the trade.[2]

Many of the problems German workers faced a century and more ago do not sound so remote or different to those that workers face today. One of the glaring omissions many make is to overlook the number of individuals working in the service industry. In an era before the almost countless mechanical devises that simplify everyday tasks, the better-off relied on servants to provide comfort in the form of meals, serving coffee, cleaning clothing and so on. These jobs were different from those in the factory or the mining pit but not necessarily better.

Doris Viersbeck, a cook and housemaid in Hamburg in the last decades of Imperial Germany, has detailed the systematic abuse she was subjected to in many wealthy homes. Although she had to rise at 6 a.m. every morning, Doris was repeatedly awoken in the middle of the night to prepare fresh coffee for her insomniac master. Cursed, threatened and bullied by employers, despite working in what may have appeared a welcome alternative to factory labor, she describes a hellish situation. In her autobiography, she pleads, "I just wanted to be treated like a human being."[3]

The resentment felt among women "in service" sometimes expressed itself in peculiar ways. Responding to questions from a pastor in 1909, a woman we know only as "Frau Hoffmann" put forth an unusual theory on the difference between the rich and servants. "There are a lot more pretty faces among the servants than in the upper classes," this retired maid argued, because the "upper classes don't get out in the air enough and they don't eat everything. Many of them have clumpy faces. Some have a nose like a fist."[4]

Another woman, whose name we don't know, went to work packing shoes in a factory where she found a co-worker who was pregnant with the unacknowledged child of a higher factory functionary. The man now rejecting his former lover, "was looking for another victim for his lust; his eyes fell on me, but he didn't have much luck because I bluntly brushed him off."[5] As a result, she was fired and back on the streets looking for work.

Although it was difficult to organize female factory workers, it was far from impossible. While more conservative male workers confidently predicted that women would never become an important part of the work force, history has proven them wrong. Women remained neither completely marginal nor impossible to organize as the rapid expansion of female trade unions from under seven thousand in 1895 to over a million in 1919 shows.[6]

Returning to our example of the discharged woman above, she later decided to become a barmaid only to find that she was subject routinely to sexual harassment from male customers. "Often I cried bitterly after the customers were all gone because I had to put up with so much ... [many asked] 'where do you live? Can I come and visit you?' And then they would try to kiss me or otherwise fondle me."[7] That her situation was far from unique among barmaids was of scant comfort.

The objection could be made that these accounts mainly came from women members of, or at least sympathetic to, German socialism. Yet, the culture of sexual predation that proletarian females suffered at the hands of the upper class is documented by middle-class, religious and anti-socialist sources. A social reformer and early bourgeois feminist, Minna Wettstein-Adelt spent three and a half months working in four different factories in Chemnitz, Saxony. She was shocked to find that working-class accusations against men of her class were justified.

The middle-class reformer noted the fanatical hatred of "ink wipers" as the factory women dubbed clerks and businessmen working in offices. As one 30-year-old woman told her, a proper factory girl "does not associate with any damned ink licker ... better the direst, blackest worker than such a vile loafer and toady!" Working beside such women, Wettstein-Adelt came to share "their sentiments wholeheartedly." It is young businessmen who "if a working girl refuses to give herself willingly to them, they use intrigue, slanderous remarks to the director, malicious suppression and harassment." The conservative female author then sighs that this pushes working women into the arms of Social Democracy since these men treat the "girls better, more politely and more humanely than others."[8] Of note is the fact that the Social Democrats were also among the earliest advocates of the legalization of homosexuality.[9]

It would be mistaken to think that unsolicited sexual advances were only a female problem. Male food servers experienced this sort of unwanted sexual harassment as well. Franz Bergg, a waiter at an expensive restaurant and casino near Danzig at the end of the nineteenth century, recalls the "not infrequent" instances of sexual stalking of waiters by "men who in their public life held important offices and were considered pillars of religion and morality."[10] Moreover, he repeatedly speaks of the hunger of waiters while they were serving copious amounts of fine food to the rich since "we weren't given at all enough to eat."[11] Of course, they were punished if caught eating the scraps left over by their well-fed customers.

Perhaps more surprising is the burning resentment Bergg felt for the system of tipping. His bitter complaint is worth quoting at length:

> We'd actually sold ourselves, sold ourselves for tips! Oh, this custom! This jingling invitation to humiliation and subjection that suppresses a free humanity! It seduces the giver into arrogance and misanthropy; and it robs the receiver of the last vestiges of human dignity. Tips are not really wages for work performed; they are compensations for special services. First you have to show yourself worthy of this dog's pay. We tried to do so by running, bowing, and fawning and with a thousand little attentions of look, manner and gesture.[12]

Still, the often-hungry wait staff had no choice but to swallow their pride along with whatever scraps they could pilfer and behave as expected.

It was little better among rural farm workers. While many farm owners lived a comfortable life, this was rarely true for the large number of landless workers who were forced to work for them. Franz Rehbein, a farm worker in Pomerania until he lost a hand in a threshing machine in 1895, paints a sad portrait of the lot of farm workers after harvest:

> None of the farmers had anything for us day laborers to do … With pent-up rage you see the prosperous farmers driving to their visits and amusements, unconcerned about the increasing misery of the day laborers … There you sit, a wretch who would gladly work; but the people for whom you've worked yourself to death for low wages in the summer are now shrugging their broad shoulders indifferently.[13]

Fritz Pauk grew up in a village that was deeply conservative. Social Democracy or any sort of radicalism was constantly attacked and turned into a monster to scare children. In fact, when he and his friends misbehaved as children, an aunt would say, "The Social Democrats are coming!" and the kids "ran away like rabbits."[14] Pauk later became less frightened of this particular ghost over time as life dealt him reasons to be less supportive of the status quo. At the age of ten, he worked for a farmer whose mistreatment cost him a foot.

He relates how around 1898–9, the winter came and "I froze in my ragged clothes. I didn't have any decent socks anymore. All I had was a crummy pair of shoes given to me by one of the farmhands ... Then one day my left foot got badly swollen ... I couldn't walk and had to stay in bed."[15] After four weeks, the farmer, at last, called a doctor and Fritz's foot had to be amputated. This limited the boy's future employment prospects and "for a long time my heart broke when I watched my chums playing, without being able to join in."[16]

Of course, having access to such narrative accounts is not the norm as few workers achieved the education needed to document them. Nonetheless, there is statistical evidence that suggests that the physical markings of class were not unique occurrences. Gottlieb Schnapper-Arndt was related to the Frankfurt branch of the Rothschild family and did not have to work for a living, nevertheless he became curious as to the condition of the common people. Among his other various scholarly studies, Schnapper-Arndt studied military draft records for a period of five years in the latter part of the nineteenth century. From this evidence, he discovered 62.3 percent of all males were rejected as unfit due to "general body weakness, hernia, varicose veins ... and other deformities."[17]

In the years before World War I, the life expectancy of average German citizens was roughly half of what it would become by the twenty-first century. In the first decade after German unification in 1871, a female at birth could look forward to only an average of 38.5 years while boy babies could expect even less with an average of 35.6 years. By 1914 this rose to 51 years for a girl baby at birth and 47 years for their male counterpart.[18] During this same period, the average working week fell from 72 hours (with mainly 12-hour days) to a 54–60 hour working week (with 10-hour days).[19]

German common people felt alienated mainly in reaction to their own exploitation but also in reaction to the exploitation they witnessed of others. The injustice of the society towards others often caused revulsion. Otto Krille, later a factory worker in Dresden, recalled his short-lived career as a scribe in a real estate office. The work seemed easy and the owners regularly gave him a glass of wine. He soon realized that the freely flowing wine "was only there to put the buyer in a good mood for the fleecing." The worst assignment for the young Krille was when he was dispatched to collect rent from a widow who had a little grocery store. "I quickly saw that she was very badly off, and when she made promises with tears in her eyes, I returned to the office empty-handed." He was sent back with a more seasoned colleague who had her serve them wine and made promises to help with the boss. A few weeks later, they closed the widow's store.[20]

Soon the real estate office also closed amid an economic downturn and Krille was out of work. He sought out employment at a textile factory, the first of many industrial jobs. His life experience had taught him a different lesson than that of the church or army. "The fate of an entire class of people was soon frighteningly clear to me," Otto Krille remembered, "Day after day, week after week, year after year, always this monotonous life with no variety. For centuries, thousands of lives had just been unwinding, like the threads on my machine."[21]

Nor was this the perception of workers alone. Krille's dire picture of industrial life was validated by the famous social scientist, Max Weber. The scholar, who was in no sense a radical, described the modern German factory as functioning with "hierarchic authority structure, its discipline, its chaining of men to machines, its spatial aggregation and yet isolation of the workers ... its formidable accounting system that reaches down to the simplest hand movement of the worker."[22] Naturally, there were important differences even within any given work place as more highly skilled workers had better wages and conditions. These better-off workers were often considered a "labor aristocracy."[23]

In fact, the German common people were always as complicated and contradictory as one would expect. One historian who examined Hamburg police informer reports that began in 1892 revealed workers were neither helpless victims nor heroic rebels but rather extremely complex individuals. They liked to gamble and could sometimes justify dishonesty by unfair treatment by their superiors. Interestingly, class identification was fundamental to them and they had a distinct suspicion of those in higher socio-economic classes. Of course, the truth of police agents is always to be suspected and their eavesdropping was limited to male workers in taverns.[24]

If work life was scarcely a pleasure for most, neither was home life. Rural conditions had always been hard except for the better off, urban living proved to be little softer. Even if wages slowly rose in the latter part of the nineteenth century, urban housing was to remain tight. Crowded and expensive, working-class families were shoe-horned into tiny, typically depressing flats. Towns over 5,000 inhabitants witnessed over 70 percent of all apartments having three or less rooms in 1910. Berlin, the German capital, was even worse with perhaps as many as three out of every ten residents living five or more people to a room.[25] A female investigator in 1913 found that Berliners not uncommonly had a home that consisted of "A living room and tiny kitchen; with two adults and three children, that means that everyone sleeps in the same room, all three children in one bed."[26]

In 1891, a Christian organization, known as the Evangelical Workers' Association of Hamburg and Karlsruhe, reported on the condition of the average workers' housing. "The landlord supplies only the essential materials and the worker then repairs the defects, without any compensation," a report from Hamburg noted; "as a rule, two families use one toilet, in some cases four to five families have to make do with one."[27] In these flats, another report from Karlsruhe commented, there is little decoration beyond some landscape art reproductions and "quite often a portrait of Lassalle [an early German Socialist leader] or [Karl] Marx, but also the first German Emperor ... [among more religious workers] pictures of saints in Catholic households—Luther portraits among Protestants."[28]

Significantly, by this period, over 99 percent of Germans were classified as literate by the government.[29] This gave commoners easy access to the radical ideas spread by socialist newspapers and booklets. Still, such miserable housing drove men to drink, women to despair and most everyone to anger. It meant that couples often found normal sexual relations difficult, if not impossible.[30] All this combined with unsatisfactory, sometimes horrific, work lives meant many families became dysfunctional with domestic violence, child neglect and all the familiar urban disorders one would suspect. The average people in Imperial Germany also changed jobs with frequency in hopes of finding a kinder boss or higher wages. In some instances this helped, usually it did not.

Sometimes they gave up completely on the industrializing Kaiser's realm and left their country for good. Overseas emigration, largely to the western hemisphere, was 626,000 for the period 1871–80, while the following decade of the anti-socialist laws saw 1,342,400 individuals biding good bye to the land of their birth. In 1891–1900, 529,000 Germans called it quits on the fatherland followed by another 279,600 emigrating in the next ten years.[31]

For others, the choice was a type of internal emigration through beer and schnapps. In Germany, the cult of sobriety was never as pervasive as in English speaking societies. This did not suggest constant intoxication, rather it was seen as one of the good things in an otherwise difficult life.[32] It was an outlet for all the many frustrations that average Germans faced. One scholar went so far as to contend that "alcohol was one of the indispensable foundations of the modern social order. Without it, contemporary social and political conditions would long since have become intolerable."[33]

Another reaction to the misery of life in Imperial Germany was to engage in petty theft. The idea of getting some of "their own back" by pilfering goods was widespread. In Hamburg, as employers ignored trade union warnings that only a living wage would prevent stealing, the docks became the source of an unofficial, and unlawful, wage supplement for many poorly paid laborers. According to Hamburg police records, the number of goods in transit that were illegally expropriated by dock workers soared from 906 in 1900 to 3,217 in 1913.[34] This is doubtlessly a severe undercount, as it does not include thefts from railroads or other means of transport. Nor would it include small amounts of food that workers ate immediately and may never have been reported.

This slide into illegality was in no way unique to Hamburg or dockworkers since crime against property was more closely related to poverty than poor morals. In a study looking at the connection between rye prices (rye was an important part of the German diet) and crimes against property in Bavaria, largely Catholic in the south, researchers found a correlation. The higher rye prices went, the more crimes against property rose.[35] A few years later, a follow up study looking at the German provinces of Prussia, largely Protestant in the north, employed this same methodology of looking at grain prices and crime rates. The result was that based on the "data for the years 1882–1910, we find a significantly positive effect of poverty on property crime."[36] In other words, neither confessional belief nor region changed the relation between poverty and property crimes.

In the decades before World War I, the German common people lived, loved, had children (legitimate or not), formed friendships and engaged in social activity. Most were straight, many were gay. Some women remained passive but many became active and resisted the old male-dominated system. They were typical humans living their lives in a myriad of ways. Some were avid revolutionaries; most were looking forward to the hope of a gradual improvement of their conditions. They were diverse in any number of ways: gender, region, religion and occupation. What they had in common, increasingly, was a shared hatred for the capitalist system in which they labored. This would result in an explosion during the pressure cooker of world war. Some must have known the verse by German poet Goethe:

> You must conquer and rule
> Or serve and lose,
> Suffer or triumph,
> Be the anvil or the hammer.[37]

Increasingly, common people decided they would rather be the hammer.

2

The Rise of Popular Radicalism

It was never preordained that masses of ordinary Germans would choose to move towards socialism.[1] Socialism, or Social Democracy as it was called in most of Europe at the time, was only one of the belief systems on offer. The common people could have doubled down on their traditional religious beliefs in hopes of a better life in the next world. They could have accepted the liberal belief that there was no alternative to capitalism, shrugged their shoulders and had another drink. Alternatively, they could have embraced the idea that the violent destruction of all existing society, and indeed the state itself, was the best reaction to oppression and become anarchists like so many people did in Italy and Spain.

With notable exceptions, German working people rejected these alternatives in favor of Social Democracy. By the last summer before World War I, Social Democracy represented the largest single force in Germany's parliament, the Reichstag. It dominated many aspects of life, particularly among urbanized working people, from politics to leisure activities. Many, not just adherents, saw it as an empire within the Imperial German Empire. But this was not always so.

In the years leading to the unification of Germany, the socialist left was small, fragmented and much harassed by the police. German Social Democracy was split into two major factions: the *Lassalleans* followed the teachings of Ferdinand Lassalle and the *Eisenachers* claimed to follow Karl Marx and Frederick Engels. These factions hated each other. When the Franco-Prussian war, (the final war that allowed German unification) broke out, the socialists found themselves on opposing sides.

In 1870, August Bebel and Wilhelm Liebknecht, who were both Eisenachers sitting in the Reichstag of the Northern German Confederation, refused to vote for war credits to pay for the war against France. Their rivals writing in the Lassallean newspaper, *Social-Demokrat*, suggested that the two Eisenacher leaders should be jailed for their opposition to the war.[2] As it turned out, they were. At this point, no one was quick to predict a bright future for German socialism. Even August Bebel, who would later be known as the "shadow Emperor" of Germany,[3] lamented, "What good did it [opposition to the war] do? The clever man gives in."[4]

All of this suggests a shaky start on the road to a united, socialist party. Nevertheless, the unification of Germany made the need for some type of united workers' party all the more urgent. In late May of 1875, at the Gotha Unity Congress, the Eisenachers and Lassalleans merged after a long series of discussions, deals and maneuvers. Karl Marx and Friedrich Engels tore this program to pieces—almost literally one suspects. Marx complained in his famous *Critique of the Gotha Program*, that the German party had revealed that its socialism was not even skin-deep, polluted by a servile belief in the state or by a belief in miracles.[5] None of this much mattered, of course, to average people.

Although it may have been weak in theory and confused in doctrine, the new party was christened the Social Democratic Party of Germany, or SPD. The party grew rapidly during the 1870s. In the 1877 election, the Socialists received 493,447 votes for 9.1 percent of the total and elected twelve members to the Reichstag.[6] This was in addition to a growing propaganda apparatus which boasted "forty-four political newspapers, one illustrated journal, a monthly and a semi-monthly review, two comic papers, and fourteen trade-union publications, in addition to *Vorwärts*, the party's official organ."[7]

The rulers did not overlook this growing power and quickly recognized the Socialists as a potential threat to their rule. In 1878, Otto von Bismarck, the so-called Iron Chancellor, convinced the Reichstag to approve restrictive laws aimed at curbing the development of socialism and the workers' movement. Within the first year of those laws being enacted, the Imperial German government had outlawed 244 associations as well as 184 periodicals and 307 non-periodical newspapers or magazines.[8]

While these figures might appear to indicate a successful crackdown, the Socialist movement kept functioning, as evidenced by the illegal distribution of the paper *Social-Demokrat*. By 1884, approximately nine thousand copies of each issue made it past police eyes and into the hands of party members and supporters.[9] Undoubtedly the initial crackdown hurt Social Democracy, but Bismarck's repression was minimal as compared to the latter total war waged by the Nazis against socialism. The anti-socialists laws of 1878 did not, for example, prevent Socialists from standing as candidates in Reichstag elections. By the 1887 balloting, the party's public image had recovered so much that 763,128 votes were cast for Socialist candidates.[10] Despite having the entire apparatus of the Imperial German Empire at his disposal, Bismarck was unable to destroy the growth of socialism among the working class.

At times, the anti-socialist laws hardened otherwise moderate socialist supporters. One woman relates how her father, a cigar worker, was arrested with eight comrades and given nine months in prison for distributing socialist literature. While he acknowledged that those were the darkest days of his life, he returned unrepentant. Rather than leave politics, his experience "prompted him to spend a lot of time in pubs in order to politicize."[11] Good for the movement, even if bad for the liver. Of course, firsthand accounts may be distorted, mistaken or simply wrong because of faulty memory. Regardless of the source and subject, these anecdotal accounts should be viewed cautiously and with an awareness of their biases.[12]

Although the repression, which continued until 1890, failed to destroy German socialism, it did push the party in a more moderate direction. Since the laws struck hardest against the most visible and articulate socialists the most radical workers tended to be the ones exiled. While many returned to Germany after the laws lapsed, others did not. Of those who did come back, many had lost their original radical temperament, having spent their exile in liberal capitalist nations like England—Eduard Bernstein[13] comes immediately to mind as an example.

At this stage in the history of the SPD, the party's Reichstag faction took on added importance. Since the Socialists elected to office were the only representatives of the party who had any freedom to work openly, these men began to regard themselves as the de facto leadership. In a letter to Liebknecht, August Bebel attacked this attitude saying that a Reichstag seat "satisfies their ambition and their vanity; with great self-complacency they look upon themselves as among the 'chosen of the nation' and find immense pleasure in the parliamentary comedy, they take it *very* seriously."[14]

With the lapse of the Anti-Socialist laws and the fall of Bismarck in 1890, Social Democracy emerged from its twelve-year-long forced semi-retirement that had prevented open agitation. As the vote totals climbed higher and higher for the Social Democrats, there was corresponding growth in the party's treasury. At the Halle Congress of 1890, it was revealed that regular receipts had more than doubled from 37,410 marks in 1880 to 95,000 marks by 1883. These shocking jumps continued with 208,655 marks collected in 1887 and the year 1890 brought in 324,322 marks, of which over one-third had been saved.[15]

Though the anti-socialist laws had lapsed, authorities still aimed to hamper any action by the SPD. Even peaceful protest was often savagely repressed. The aim of the authorities was to intimidate those who might oppose the system. As was mentioned before, the result of this repression could be the opposite with some people becoming radicalized. Take for example Toni Sender who was a young middle-class woman in Frankfurt already drifting towards socialist beliefs in the years before World War I. One day she decided to attend a march demanding a more democratic electoral system despite both her age and gender precluding her from the right to vote.

As the protest moved through the city, armed police attacked the march and began beating people. "What have we done?" the rather naïve young woman shouted. "Is the street forbidden to the tax-paying citizen?" Not atypically, the "answer was a rain of blows. My back hurt terribly. Never in my life had I been so furious." She made a vow that day to fight for "a free citizenry in a city and a country liberated from the rule of the feudal barons and their brutal mercenaries."[16] Sender went on to become a socialist member of the Reichstag[17] and she was certainly not the only one whose experiences with political repression fostered their radicalism.

All the same, the majority of people do not live by politics alone. Nor do they exist only for work, however essential and formative their work might be. They lived, loved, played, had friends and did all the other things that make people human. In most societies, this means interacting with a civil society whose institutions are created and run in the interests of the status quo. These include Churches that insists you render unto Caesar, harmless festivals organized by the upper classes, sports clubs considered a useful distraction by the rulers, schools that teach obedience and proper social and gender roles. That is, a wealth of institutions that spread the ideas and norms that mold people into obedient citizens.

So it is most times and most everywhere throughout history. In pre-World War I Germany there was a clear challenge to the existing norms and practices of society. German socialism competed for primacy not just in politics but also in the structuring of social and cultural practices. Socialists were involved in the lives of the citizens not just during elections or labor struggles but also during people's leisure time. As Ruth Fischer, a one-time radical critic, conceded, German Social Democracy "became a way of life. It was much more than a political machine; it gave the German worker dignity and status in a world of his own. The individual worker lived in his party, the party penetrated into workers' everyday habits. His ideas, his reactions, his attitudes, were formed out of this integration of his person with his collective."[18] In an effort to understand the far-reaching social and cultural influence of the socialist party, historians pore over the pages of the SPD theoretical journal, *Die Neue Zeit* (the New Age), which claimed to advance Marxist theory. Doubtlessly, this is a useful way to estimate intellectual currents within the German left.

Yet, less remarked upon is the wide range and hefty memberships of organizations not so directly focused on politics, let alone concerned with weighty ideological issues.[19] This was reflected in a virtual forest of popular publications. Thus, a radical intellectual could spend the evening perusing the pages of *Die Neue Zeit* while less theoretically oriented workers could spend their free time with *Der Arbeiter Radfahrer* (Worker Cyclist) or the *Arbeiter Turnzeitung* (Worker Gymnastic Newspaper). Even socialist innkeepers and stenographers had their own publications.[20] If a worker wanted to borrow a novel, there were worker libraries.[21] Those who wished to sing could join "red" singing societies. For those who enjoyed beer, there were frequent meetings and dinners in beer halls while others could join the German Workers Temperance Federation. So, the German common people could socialize at taverns, the work floor, picnics, choirs, gymnastic clubs, chess clubs, public lectures or book readings.

Naturally, the government kept a concerned eye on all of these less than discreet activities. Some of these organizations were so apolitical on the surface that the rulers didn't think it necessary, or advisable, to restrict them. Many were mainly sports and recreation organizations such as the Friends of Nature Walking Association, Workers' Swimming Association, Free Sailing Union, Free Shooting Association or the Workers' Chess Union. In fact, Germany led the world in workers sports in terms of membership and level of activity.[22] Intellectuals of the Marxist persuasion have argued that the popularity of worker-competitions was produced by the alienation common people felt under the pressures of industrial capitalism. Regardless of causes, sports was a field of contention between the socialist-oriented workers, church sponsored clubs and the paternalism of the middle class.[23]

These organizations also gave ordinary Germans the chance at an alternative identity. "A working-class family could purchase its groceries at the socialist cooperative, borrow books from the Social Democratic library, exercise at a workers' sports club, sing in the workers' choir, if necessary call on the workers Samaritan Association in the event of an accident," as Lynn Abrams has noted, "and draw on the workers' burial fund upon the death of a family member."[24] This was all very important because it developed an alternative culture in which members helped construct the notion of what is meant to be a Social Democrat. Another historian wrote, "Sociability, and all frivolities that implied, could not be cast aside without undermining the whole structure. Personal attachment, familiarity, and fellowship among acquaintances created emotional bonds that were just as important for the vitality of the cultural world of the labor movement as party loyalty and ideological commitment."[25]

Now to some, this may not seem very important. How did chess clubs or picnics advance opposition to Germany's ruling elites? A question many might well ask. Vladimir Lenin, who later became the head of Bolshevik Russia, took time out during the Balkan wars[26] that preceded World War I, to wax enthusiastically about these organizations. In 1913, the Russian radical applauded the German workers' choir societies for "a kind of jubilee: the number of worker-singers reached 100,000, with a total membership of 165,000," while when founded in the 1860s "there were 12 members" and "no amount of police harassment can prevent the singing of the hearty proletarian song."[27] Lenin was right. All these activities served a number of important functions. They created a sense of belonging—a feeling of solidarity among people who otherwise might have been isolated or demoralized. They allowed for the informal exchange of idea and emotions. After all, the evidence suggests "socialist ideas spread among workers far more effectively by word of mouth ... than through individual readings."[28] As institutions, they were a counterweight to rulers, state and churches.

Lenin was not alone in thinking that these associations were institutions that built up class consciousness; so did the German authorities. One author details the situation in 1890s Hamburg, the "political police sent plain-clothes agents to meetings that were not open to the public and built up an elaborate system of secret surveillance over bars and pubs known to be the haunt of Social Democrats and other radicals. It backed up the information it acquired in this way with a systematic monitoring of the local and national press ... [the rulers were] not only seriously alarmed by the threat from below, but also unusually well informed about it as well."[29] The authorities were particularly worried about the printed word. One Social Democratic journalist, August Otto-Walster tried to popularize radical ideas by means of plays and novels. His major novel, *At the Loom of Time: A Social-political Novel*, in the words of the police, had heroes [who] "in their speeches and in their conversations, translate the doctrines of socialist theoreticians into everyday language." The work was banned because the popular novel's purpose was "to disseminate the most essential doctrines and allegations of the Social Democrats and Communists to the widest possible circle in an easy and accessible—and therefore doubly effective—form."[30] This novel spread widely and illegally; some historians speculate that the ban actually increased people's desire to get hold of a copy.

In Berlin, a *Free People's Theatre* was founded in 1890 to enhance popular class awareness with dramas that were cutting edge critiques of the status quo.[31] It was popular with average people and extremely well attended but was censored whenever it presented more blatantly political fare. One such play, modeled on Zola's *Germinal*, titled *Those Who Live in the Shadows*, told the story of impoverished miners being heartlessly exploited by a powerful and corrupt family of mine owners supported by the Church. It was banned and the theatre appealed to the courts. In January 1914 the court ruled that people viewing the play would be agitated, inflamed and provoked while "filling them with a deep embitterment and hatred against the entrepreneurial class, [but also the Church,] state and society that allows such [exploitive] conditions to exist." In addition to Berlin, the play was banned in Hanover yet performed in Stuttgart, Frankfurt and other cities.[32]

Did people understand the root causes of systemic realities, or what could be done to change them? After all, did anyone among the German masses read Karl Marx's *Das Kapital?* Some indeed did. A seamstress recalled helping her father smuggle forbidden books into their home. Afterwards, her father "read aloud and we discussed while I sewed. We spent a whole year reading Marx['s] *Kapital.*"[33] This was far from typical though and we should not imagine most workers coming home from ten or twelve hours at work to anxiously curl up with a copy of Marx's *Theories of Surplus Value.* From the evidence culled from worker libraries and socialist party records, it seems most people did not spend a year of their time going through *Das Kapital.*[34] This may miss the point, however.

Few workers read Charles Darwin's *Origins of the Species* either. With Darwin as with Marx, that most ordinary Germans did not actually read the texts themselves did not prevent them from accepting the general ideas proposed. Marx's main ideas were popularized through pamphlets and even fiction, as noted before. Interestingly, *Origin of the Family, Private Property and the State* by Engels was quite popular although few may have read the entire original work. Also widely read by German workers was *Women Under Socialism* by SPD founder August Bebel.[35] Did most common people understand any of these works on the level that would pass a University examination? Of course not. Did they impart certain ideas that challenged the existing political, economic and social system of Imperial Germany? Yes, as one historian has argued, "their rejection of capitalism and the prevailing class system was sincere ... However vaguely, they envisioned a future where exploitation, selfishness, and cruelty had disappeared."[36]

One basic indication of how people felt about their situation was their willingness to go out on strike. Strikes took place despite scant legal protection, brutal police repression and loss of income that pushed many a family to the brink of starvation. Given the massive institutional resistance a strike would face, why did people risk going out? Causes included frustration, sometimes despair, and often a desperate desire for a better life. Furthermore, sometimes the strikers won. Aurelia Roth, a female glass grinder, described how her co-workers "talked a lot about how it couldn't go on much longer like this. Something had to be done to put a stop to these goings-on ... a man said that if Social Democracy didn't take a hand in making way for better conditions, it wouldn't be long before typhus and starvation would break out."[37] As one would expect, women glassworkers were typically paid half the wages of their male counterparts.

So the glassworkers organized a union and demanded the owners grant a minimum wage. Unsurprisingly, the proprietors didn't take the workers' demands very seriously. In response, the glassworkers went out on strike. Roth details what followed, "Within half an hour the machines stopped all over town. The strikers marched from one workshop to the next, and everyone joined the parade. We marched to neighboring towns. In one grinding mill where the workers refused to stop work, everything was smashed ... The strike was supposed to be general. When the owners saw that the people would no longer work under the old conditions, they began to negotiate and they agreed to almost all of our demands."[38] As can be seen from Table 2.1, such strikes were far from rare although the outcome was not always so positive for the strikers.

These struggles helped increase real wages, reduce the number of working hours and generally improve working conditions. However, the employers responded by increasing the intensity of work, often through the introduction of new technology. Furthermore, if the German common people made gains in the decades before World War I, the possessing classes made even greater gains. When increased productivity and enhanced profits are taken into account, the *relative wages*, which is the percentage of production that went to the employees, actually went down. As one economic historian comments, the "relative income of the workers in 1914 was only about one-third of what it was in 1860. The rich had become enormously richer and the national wealth of Germany had grown, but the workers' share in this wealth had declined rapidly. The relative deterioration of the workers had proceeded at a speed probably unsurpassed in any country in Europe."[39] Did most average Germans understand these economic complexities? Unlikely. Did many common people know they were being had? Ja.

Even a quick glance at Table 2.1 draws the eye to the year 1905 with its huge number of strikes, strikers and days of labor lost. The Russian Revolution of 1905 provided a prime example of revolutionary success to ordinary citizens at a time when German industrialization was intensifying. The combination of this unexpected rebellion in the land of the Czars with a massive strike in the Ruhr region of northwest Germany produced a powerful reaction from the German working class.[40] The rising of the Russian peoples helped initiate massive demonstrations of workers by the thousands who demanded equal suffrage in marches in Dresden, Chemnitz, Plauen and other Saxon cities.[41] In Hamburg, where the local administration had prepared new regulations to prevent a Socialist "takeover" of the state government, SPD leaders issued calls for meetings. Little did they expect that thousands would spontaneously walk off their jobs.[42] This was not only the first significant political strike since 1848–49 but also "qualifies as the first general strike in German history."[43]

In 1912, Adolf Levenstein published *The Working Class Question*, wherein he attempted to show the world the living thoughts and hopes of his fellow workers.[44] Although there were methodological problems and flaws in his survey, as exist in all such imprecise instruments seeking to take a snap shot of something as complex as human consciousness, Levenstein distributed 8,000

Table 2.1   Total number of workers involved in strikes (no "political strikes" collected until 1911), consisting of blue-collar workers, 1899–1914

Year	Number of strikes	Establishments affected	Maximum number of workers simultaneously striking	Total amount of "working days lost"
1899	1,288	7,121	109,460	3,265,881
1900	1,433	7,740	131,810	3,188,654
1901	1,056	4,561	62,682	2,311,573
1902	1,060	3,437	60,184	1,326,833
1903	1,374	7,000	99,414	2,815,491
1904	1,870	10,321	120,268	3,622,998
1905	2,403	14,481	420,160	14,536,233
1906	3,328	16,246	296,651	8,176,337
1907	2,266	13,092	203,024	6,204,558
1908	1,347	4,774	75,797	2,258,944
1909	1,537	4,811	107,055	2,812,876
1910	2,113	8,276	167,908	4,582,036
1911	2,566	10,640	238,165	7,731,334
1912	2,510	7,255	417,407	7,711,764
1913	2,127	9,007	265,575	8,819,351
1914	1,115	5,213	61,304	1,756,509

Source: data from K. Tenfelde and H. Volkmann, *Streik: Zur Geschichte des Arbeitskampfes in Deutschland während der Industrialisierung*, Munich: Beck, 1981: 304–13.

questionnaires and had a high 63 percent rate of return. Many of the responses were what one would expect. Thus, between a quarter and a third of the people questioned about their hopes and wishes said they wanted to earn more money. One 46-year-old steelworker simply wrote, "I hope for better conditions of life and a carefree old age." This sentiment would be as common today as in 1912. What was striking was that almost the same percentage hoped for "the victory of the Social Democrats" and one in six gave an answer considered "utopian." A striking six percent put forth that their most important wish was to "settle accounts with the capitalists."[45] This suggests a highly politicized working class had grown up as Imperial Germany industrialized.

Most workers hoped for a gradual improvement typically accomplished in part by electoral victories of the SPD. Interestingly, a significant minority of slightly over twelve percent of those questioned appear to be hardened revolutionaries or "utopians" as Levenstein termed them. Their responses were far from the typical hope for higher wages or better conditions. For example, a 32-year-old miner wrote, "My foremost wish is to carry the banner when the war against the capitalists and the Junkers comes, and to mow them down to the last man."[46] Of course, the great majority clung to the idea of a gradual, peaceful road to reform and socialism but it is important to note the existence of such a radical minority. The views of even the more moderate majority might be off-putting to a conservative. After all, only 25 percent believed in a supreme being and even then a great number did not seem to have in mind a Christian god. When asked about reading habits it was not just that few read the Bible but rather that 40 percent "reported reading primarily socialist books and trade union literature."[47]

In the end, the German common people, and certainly their most politically active members, simply did not believe that they lived in the best of all possible worlds. They may have been told that, in the words of the late Lady Thatcher, "there is no alternative." They nonetheless thought things could be made better. German commoners, by and large, simply refused to believe that a better world wasn't possible. Certainly different people had conflicting views of what that better world would look like. But, what united huge numbers was that they knew that the world they lived in was not their ideal. This in no way guaranteed revolution. A slow dripping of reforms could have placated the common people while giving away as little real power as possible. Let radicals have office as long as they didn't have real power. After all, that is basically how ruling classes in other nation-states have played their cards. It might have been that way in Germany, too. But, then as Otto von Bismarck had warned "some fool thing in the Balkans" happened and Germany was drawn into a world war. Of course, the real causes behind the war are much more complex and numerous than the mere assassination of an Austrian aristocrat.[48] World War I erupted and war would turn out to be the handmaiden of revolution.

World War I is typically portrayed with descriptions of joyful German male youth marching off, happy women draping flowers over them as they went by. That these scenes occurred on occasion is doubtlessly true. However, the common people's reaction to war was far more complex. With the outbreak of war, one German soldier remembered marching off with his unit past female friends, lovers and relatives to the railroad station that would take them to the front. But, he drew a far different picture than the idyllic scenes typically reported in the controlled press and repeated in historical mythology. The soldier, Julius Koettgen, told of desperate women clinging to their men, some having to be removed by force. It was as if the women, "had a vision of the fate of their beloved ones, as if they were beholding the silent graves in foreign lands to which those poor nameless ones were to be buried, they sought to cling fast to their possession, to retain what already no longer belonged to them."[49] This story would appear to contradict the received wisdom of massive pro-war feeling among Germans.

Recent research has led some historians to argue that the idea of general German enthusiasm for war in 1914 is one of the major historical myths of the twentieth century. The press, the government and the military did everything to encourage pro-war sentiment and stage managed demonstrations and photo ops. So the rally of 50,000 pro-war Germans in Berlin in August 1, 1914 is highlighted while the anti-war demonstrations of 100,000–200,000 in Berlin only some days before are forgotten.[50] Historians now estimate that as many as 1,000,000 across Germany took to the streets in July 1914 to protest the prospect of war.[51]

3
War, Suffering and Resistance

In no other nation, did so many try to prevent their government from going to war than in Germany.[1] In fact, the common people of Germany had repeatedly protested against war in the years before World War I.[2] Even the more conservative rural population was mainly against war if for no other reason than the farmers feared losing their harvests.[3]

Certainly, there were signs of war fever "but in most cases, officials seem to have been the moving spirits in the noble enterprise of encouraging the people."[4] True, crowds gathered in Berlin to cheer the Kaiser and his wife but their enthusiasm was no greater than in peacetime. It is also true that the leaders of German Social Democracy lined up to support the government and voted for war credits but there is scant evidence that this was because of war's popularity among their rank and file members.[5]

Even within the SPD, there were many who thought that this move, often motivated as a way to protect the party's property and legality, was wrong. While many must have accepted the idea that this was a defensive battle against Russian Czarism, a lot of people were at very least skeptical. "We have no sympathy for Tsar and Cossack," wrote the *Leipziger Volkszeitung*, "but beware when the paper of the German industry barons talks of 'half-Asiatic hordes of Cossacks rushing over German frontiers'."[6] The same Socialist newspaper argued, "in the first days the government did nothing to secure peace."

Although still a distinct minority within the German Social Democratic Party, opposition to the pro-war policy of the leadership spread almost daily to larger circles of the labor movement. This development found expression in December

1914 when the Kaiser needed another 5,000,000,000 marks in war credits. As in August, the SPD Reichstag faction gathered to discuss a joint response. As before, the majority remained in favor of funding the war. Yet, those in opposition had grown from 14 to 17. Karl Liebknecht requested permission to cast an independent vote against war credits, arguing that to do otherwise would violate party resolutions and principle. Naturally, this demand was rejected.

On December 2, 1914, the Reichstag assembled and loyally voted their Kaiser more money; this time though there was one dissenter. Over the objections of his faction, including many of the minority, Liebknecht voted "No" when war credits were put to a vote. Moreover, he dispatched a memorandum to the President of the Reichstag explaining his vote by condemning the war as an imperialist adventure seeking conquest.[7] This stand would make Liebknecht one of the symbols of the peace movement as even government censorship could not hide his dissent.

Another widely held myth is that the leaders of Germany had no reason, until late in the war, to think they would be defeated. In the most extreme version of this so-called "stab in the back" theory, Nazis and other far rightists made the argument that Germany would have won World War I had it not been for traitors at home. This is simply untrue.

The German high command under General Erich von Falkenhayn, Chief of the German General staff, planned to strike a fast and fatal blow at France in the west while holding off Russia and other enemies in the East. This plan, basically a repeat of Prussia's successful strategy in the Franco-Prussian War of 1870–71, depended on the capture of Paris, destruction of the French army and surrender of France before significant numbers of British or other allied troops could engage the German troops.

When the French were able to halt the German offensive and the war bogged down into trench warfare in the fall of 1914, everything changed. At that point, Imperial Germany could have negotiated a favorable treaty in return for the evacuation of occupied French, Belgian and Russian territory. What they could no longer hope for was a quick victory or, in fact, any real likelihood of victory at all. This is more than mere hindsight as von Falkenhayn, himself, understood Germany's inability to win a war of attrition, fought in the trenches.

As Chief of the German General Staff, von Falkenhayn prophetically informed the Chancellor on November 18, 1914 that "as long as Russia, France and England hold together, it will be impossible for us to beat our enemies such that we will get an acceptable peace. We would instead run the danger of slowly exhausting ourselves."[8] His warning was ignored and he later engaged in a desperate throw of the dice by attacking Verdun in the vain hope that so many French soldiers would die that France would be forced to sue for peace. When his bloody sacrifice of hundreds of thousands of German lives, and a more or less equal number of French souls, failed to force France's surrender, he was removed from his position.

Realizing that the leader of the German Army knew the war was almost certainly unwinnable redeems the "defeatism" of many an average German soldier. Some at least dimly understood the military balance of power while others just had a gut feeling, but many who could resist the nationalist propaganda came to the same conclusion as General von Falkenhayn. The war was lost before Christmas 1914 and any further death and suffering served no purpose, not even for the pro-war "patriots."

Increasingly some German soldiers took matters into their own hands. William Hermanns, a disillusioned volunteer stationed at Verdun, recalls the whispered slogan making the rounds in the trenches, "A bullet from the rear is just as good as a bullet from the front." In other words, the soldiers were questioning why "a rifle could not be turned against our own superiors."[9] Although he knew a German bullet was waiting for his Lieutenant, Hermanns never said a word of warning.[10] It all seems counter to the spirit of service but demonstrates the doubt and desperation felt by the troops knowing that their commanders were persisting in an unjustifiable effort. Maybe, the German rulers persisted to save their honor—a word much beloved by the upper classes when they have no other way of explaining why the common people must suffer.

The following anecdote demonstrates just how little confidence German soldiers held in their leaders. During the battle of the Somme, a British Sergeant by the name of Dawson became hopelessly stuck in the mud. As he began to despair of rescue he was found by a party of five German soldiers, whom Dawson assumed would take him prisoner and back to their trenches. Instead, they informed him "that they were his prisoners and demanded to be taken across to our [British] trenches." Dawson got lost but all turned out well as the Germans knew the way.[11]

Still, the major media was printing the most outrageous falsehoods to do everything to promote the spirit of nationalism. Naturally, this had an effect. One later middle-class radical recalls in his autobiography, the sort of things he had heard: Germany had been bombed by the French; the country had already been invaded. He admitted, "I swallowed it all."[12] Nor was he alone in initial support for the Kaiser's war.

Richard Stumpf was as ordinary sailor who had enlisted in 1912 and served on the *Helgoland* for six years. He was a devoted Catholic, nationalistic, conservative and a monarchist. In autumn 1914, he wrote bitterly in his diary about England and her allies:

> Without shame our enemies have treated us in an unimaginably abominable and cowardly fashion. They have cut our telegraph cable to inundate the world with a flood of lies. They have attacked our defenseless colonies and have destroyed everything that German industry and technology have created.[13]

He was not to be easily swayed in his views.

For a time, many believed that the war was defensive and would be brief. Rapidly, it became clear that the war was not defensive and would not be brief. It was not long before that belief began to fade into doubt and later complete disbelief. Once the reality of modern warfare became apparent, even those who had supported the war began to question it. In fact, evidence shows that many German soldiers became disillusioned while the German army was still advancing toward Paris and a quick victory seemed likely. An officer in the German Second Reserve wrote in his diary that although several quick victories had been won there was no conqueror pride among his men. They believed the stories of the French committing atrocities against German soldiers were told to keep them "from staying behind or from going over to the French."[14]

One the other hand, that is not to say that no one defected to the pro-war camp. For one, Lily Braun who had been a socialist and a feminist abandoned her radical views and went on a pro-war speaking tour in 1914. By 1915, she was turning out "patriotic kitsch for a wartime audience in Germany."[15] But accounts such as Braun's appear to be far from typical. The most well-known women of the SPD—Rosa Luxemburg, Clara Zetkin, Käte Dunker[16] and Luise Zietz—immediately opposed the war. There is also evidence that the majority of readers of *Gleichheit*, the socialist women's publication, sided with the radical anti-war group.[17] As the war was being declared, Zetkin had used the pages of *Gleichheit* to thunder against the conflict. "War is standing before the gate. Let us drive it back into the night ..." Zetkin wrote, "Leave your factories and workshops, your huts and attics to join the mass protest!"[18] Zetkin's call to protest went unanswered until much later on.

On the home front, the successful British naval blockade prevented ships from reaching German ports. This meant that Germany quickly ran low on even basic foodstuffs. By October 1914, only a few months into the war, bread and potatoes became scarce in Germany's capital city. This scarcity caused their prices to skyrocket.[19] By winter, there were bread riots across Germany's major urban areas.

On February 16, 1915, Officer Rhein of the Berlin police reported on one riot that broke out over the sale of potatoes. As the sale began, "everyone stormed the market stands. The police, who were trying to keep order, were simply overrun and were powerless against the onslaught."[20] This was not the unique situation of the German capital. Reports from neutral Amsterdam on February 26, 1915 claimed that the bread riots were widespread, the rich were travelling to Scandinavia to get bread, and at Maddenburg, "women and children endeavored to loot the shops" only to be suppressed by the police.[21]

The situation was not much better for most of the rural population. They had an easier time coming by food but nonetheless found themselves at the mercy of government officials and the larger landowners. They watched their sons conscripted and their horses confiscated by the military. However, despite the continuation of deep class divisions and obvious suffering among the poor peasantry, the main target of rural frustration was vented at "the city people" rather than the existing social order.

Thus, the very real class tension that existed in the countryside was deflected into conservative, not radical, directions. This caused real consequences during the German Revolution. The war, therefore, "split German society into two groups—producers and consumers," at least in the mind of most German farmers.[22]

Meanwhile, there was evidence that many average German troops were different from the war-crazed machines of popular legend. Toni Sender reports on the soldiers' attitudes she observed during the first year of the war. Riding in a train full of Germans headed for the front, she saw that most were "not too enthusiastic about fighting."[23] After deciding to help with the wounded behind the lines, Sender was shocked not just by the physical injuries she witnessed but also by the typical attitude. "Most of the wounded, it was plain, were mighty glad to be out of the trenches and not eager for their wounds to heal too quickly. *Heimatschuss*—homeland shot—they used to call a more serious wound that kept them for a long period in the hospital far behind the front."[24]

Morale was further undermined as the high command was unable to prevent the spread of rumors and gossip. Even in the first months of the great conflict, latrine chatter was often far from the bellicose nationalism the officers would have liked. Word spread about how soldiers "had mutinied in such-and-such a place, in so-and-so they had been fraternizing with the French, here they'd poured the coffee on the ground in front of a general, and there a soldier had shot an officer in the line."[25]

Rumors such as these disclosed a growing reality that rank and file soldiers did not support the war, and would act out accordingly. One soldier recalls how over time they became friendly with the Russians in the opposite trenches. Once when the Russians failed to get resupplied and were on the brink of starvation, they sent a representative with a white flag and begged for food. After the initial shock, sacks were "filled with the gifts of our soldiers to the enemy—pieces of bread and biscuits with here and there a slice of bacon or a lump of cheese, all thrown *pele-mele* together. Many a man must have parted with his last piece of bread in order not to be outdone by the others …"[26]

Still, some officers had a real bloodlust as when during the initial invasion of France in 1914, a group of them shrieked, "No quarter!" The German soldiers were told to kill defenseless French troops who had thrown away their rifles while trying to surrender. If any German hesitated, their superiors squawked, "Cut them all down!" This sort of senseless slaughter did not sit well with many of the German enlisted men. The result was that some of "the 'gentlemen' who had ordered us to massacre our French comrades were killed 'by mistake' in the darkness of the night, by their own people, of course. Such 'mistakes' repeat themselves almost daily."[27] This was not caused by the frustration of defeat; at the time, the Germans were winning the war and even hardened anti-war soldiers thought they'd be in Paris before years end.

Sometimes an average soldier could not contain his anger and wait for the chance of a "mistake." Once, when an officer forced French POWs to remain in the open while shells were raining down, cries of "shame" came from the German troops. One socialist in the ranks lost his composure completely. He cried out, "That's the noble sentiment of an exploiter; that fellow is the son of an Elberfeld capitalist and his father is a sweating-den keeper of the worse sort ... [he] is murdering our own brothers!" Before he could say more he was arrested and led off but not before he threw down his gun with great force.[28]

As the first advances of the war bogged down, all sides dug themselves into trenches, often very close to the opposing forces. Despite each government's best efforts, pro-war propaganda did not always win over all those fighting. Since the trenches were often within hailing distance of each other, there is evidence that direct "communication of friendly sentiments was not uncommon."[29] Missing from many dominant narratives of World War I is the reality of frequent "live and let live" agreements whereby average soldiers simply refused to engage in, what they saw as, senseless sniping.[30] One writer put it this way: "on many occasions tacit agreements existed between the opposing troops to restrict offensive activity."[31]

Having originally been told the war would be over by Christmas of 1914, German troops were among the millions disappointed by what now seemed more like an endless conflict. Their enhanced cynicism was reflected in the increasingly bitter German soldier slang. The troops called themselves both *Kanonenfutter* (Cannon Fodder)[32] and *Frontschwein* (front pigs) because of the feeling that their lives were considered irrelevant.[33] The use of the term *Viehtrieb* (cattle drive) also demonstrates that soldiers felt they were treated like animals by those in authority.[34] Around the start of Christmas, very strange things happened in numerous places along the fronts.[35] After spending months attempting to kill each other, many soldiers decided that there should be a Christmas truce.

The following account is from a British private on the night of the Christmas truce. It began with the Germans singing "Silent Night" and placing out a sign that read "Merry Christmas." The British responded by joining in the singing. German soldiers waved their hands above the trench tops and yelled, "Happy Noel, Tommy." Then, according to the British private's account, a "German took a chance and jumped up on top of the trench and shouted out 'Happy Christmas, Tommy!' No one fired a shot … Of course our boys said, 'If he can do it, we can do it.' The sergeant major came along and said, 'Get down there, get down there.' We stuck our two fingers up at him. 'It's Christmas!' and with that we all jumped up and the Germans beckoned us forward to the barbed wire and we shook hands."[36]

It was this shared Christian heritage that allowed for these soldiers to reach out to one another for a brief truce. But, on another part of the front, German troops were quite angry that the enemy kept shooting at them on December 24. What the Germans were unaware of was that they were stationed opposite a unit of Algerians, fighting in the French army, whose faith was Islam. Alfred Kornitzke, a determined pastry chef from Berlin, refused to accept the rejection of the truce. Screaming "No one can do this to me," Kornitzke grabbed a Christmas tree and lifted it high above his head, which was covered by a white baker's cap, and ran towards the Arab soldiers. "The Algerians were baffled by the apparition, for the German appeared too crazy to shoot at and too comical to take seriously."[37] After that, the Algerians honored the truce.

The truce allowed more than just a brief ceasefire; during the truce enemies wandered tentatively into "no man's land" to exchange greetings, gifts and even play sports together. Not surprisingly, soldiers felt "a reluctance to begin shooting again and in some places the truce lasted several days."[38] None of this warmed the hearts of the staff Generals back in Berlin. Within a few days, the high command forbade all fraternization and branded approaches to enemy troops the crime of high treason.[39] Furthermore, accounts about the Christmas truce was censored from the news by Imperial Germany as well as by the other warring nations. In fact, historians also mainly ignored narratives about these events until very recently.

Now, historians accept not only that this Christmas truce happened but also acknowledge it was far wider spread than previously thought.[40] Despite every attempt to prevent it, there was still some limited fraternization by German troops during the Christmastime of the following year.[41] There were many informal truces at Christmas and troops on the Eastern Front found that Russians troops had left many Christmas trees in no man's land wishing "Merry Christmas, and hope we can come to a peaceful agreement as soon as possible."[42]

The assumption of authors and historians has been that the furious efforts of the high commands of all the nations to suppress these actions were successful. With fraternization now deemed high treason, its consequences included potential for the death penalty; naturally, open fraternization decreased as a result. This should not be taken to indicate increased morale or dedication to the cause on the part of German troops. Though they could not disobey direct orders to attack, many German soldiers in the trenches still made a mockery of the fighting.

They turned to "ritualized aggression," where troops might make a noisy show of firing off their rifles. Thus what an "outsider might perceive as a small battle, entirely consistent with the active front policy, might be in fact merely a structure of ritualized aggression, where missiles symbolized benevolence not malevolence, and where the constant flow of ritualized bombs and bullets caused neither anxiety nor harm."[43] It is much easier to fire off rounds if your goal is to miss the enemy rather than hit him.

At times, when the officers on duty were sympathetic, German infantry could dispense with even the charade of wanting to kill the enemy. There were entire sections of the trenches where there was an unspoken understanding between German and British soldiers not to needlessly shed blood. Because of these informal agreements, narrative accounts recount some curious situations. For example, a Scottish soldier stationed on the Western Front misappropriated the daily rum ration one day. The Scot "staggered drunkenly into no-man's-land and lurched along the battalion's front, all the while taking frequent swigs from a stone jar containing the rum. The inebriated Jock was in full view of the Germans who not only refrained from fire, but also laughed and cheered him along." An officer reports that, in another section of the front, two British soldiers got in a huge fight. They jumped out of the trench and fought bare fisted for 15 minutes until one was knocked out. As the officer reported, "all the time the Germans were cheering and firing their rifles in the air to encourage the combatants."[44]

These accounts are rare, comical reprieves from the usual horror of the battlefront. If the first year of the war on the German home front was horrible, the months and years that followed were even worse. This applied to average Germans, both in and out of uniform. Much praised Prussian efficiency was unable to make a ration system work when food shortages mounted. The success of the British naval blockade quickly depleted German food stocks. Imperial Germany had no plan for feeding its people in case of a long war. Before the war was six months old, the German nation was forced to ration bread flour at 225 grams per person. This ration soon went down to 200 grams and, after some fluctuation, dipped repeatedly before reaching a nadir of 160 grams in the last months of 1917–18. That is, rations were set at one-half of the estimated per capita consumption of pre-war years.[45]

Eggs were so scarce that, according to one report, in Berlin "it was possible to issue only one egg per head of population in several weeks or months."[46] Germans could no longer drown their sorrows; 95 percent of the grain normally utilized for brewing beer was diverted to other wartime uses.[47] In 1916 there was an attempt to remedy the beer problem by adding saccharine to the brew. But this adulteration was deeply resented by the people "as saccharine almost ruins a good beer."[48]

The food crisis was so great that it drastically reduced the consumption of virtually all foodstuffs with the exception of potatoes. Since the German government kept ration records, it is possible to determine the food intake for the later years of the war with reasonable accuracy. German economist Jürgen Kuczynski has compiled the statistics shown in Table 3.1.

The rationing system, said to ensure equality of sacrifice, soon became a symbol of class rations. Throughout the war, there was an extensive black market that ensured that the wealthy, the rulers and the well-connected could continue to dine in abundance and luxury. Rations were consistently reduced causing class hatred, particularly among women trying to feed their families, to grow stronger. The result was often bread riots, which were little reported in the government-censored press.

Officer Krupphausen of the Berlin police describes this scene from October 17, 1915: "the crowd had already stormed several

Table 3.1 Food rations as a percentage of peacetime consumption, 1916–18

Commodity	July 1, 1916 to June 30, 1917	July 1, 1917 to June 30, 1918	July 1, 1918 to December 28, 1918
Meat	31	20	12
Fish	51	?	5
Eggs	18	13	13
Lard	14	11	7
Butter	22	21	28
Cheese	3	4	15
Rice	4	—	—
Cereals	14	1	7
Potatoes	71	94	94
Vegetable fats	39	41	17
Milling products	53	47	48

Source: Jürgen Kuczynski, *Die Geschichte der Lage der Arbeiter Unter Dem Kapitalismus*, vol. IV, Berlin: Akademie Verlag, 1967: 351.

butter shops because of prices ... Several large display windows were shattered, shop doors destroyed, and entire stocks were simply taken ... the police and officers were completely helpless against the crowd." While mounted police cleared the street various "objects such as flower pots were thrown at us."[49]

Meanwhile, for the rich and well-connected matters were quite different. As an English woman who was married to a German nobleman wrote in her diary in late 1915, officers on leave joined in dinners where "Pheasant served on slices of pine-apple, with champagne is a mere item on a long menu."[50] Front-line soldiers also caught wind of the upper-class lifestyle that belied the myth of shared sacrifice. One soldier coming back from furlough compared the common people's food stuff, the troop rations and the way the rulers lived. He claimed to have discovered that "vaults and cellars of the Imperial Castle in Berlin had been filled with mountains of canned foods while his own family was starving."[51] Whether he knew, heard rumors, or guessed, his summation was correct.

The plethora of food substitutes introduced by the rulers of Imperial Germany could hardly have failed to add insult to injury. Designed to maintain the illusion of a normal diet, these substitutes contained little of food value. Though their numbers multiplied as the war progressed, the substitutes continued to be of poor quality and dubious taste. As one study of Imperial Germany during the war observed:

Meat was substituted by rice lamb chop, the nut cutlet, the vegetable beefsteak—a pale green concoction of cornmeal, spinach, potatoes and group nuts bound with egg—or sausages made from starch and offal. Butter was "stretched" by a powder made from starch and sodium carbonate, or replaced by a mixture of curdled milk, sugar and coloring material ... Many attempts were made to develop substitutes for fat—an abiding deficiency—from rats, mice, hamsters, crows, cockroaches, snails and earthworms, even hair clippings and old leather boots, but none was very successful. Sand and plaster of Paris were utilized for the "mineralization" of foods.[52]

People most likely found little solace in their vegetable beefsteaks or in the argument of the *Vossische Zeitung* (People's Newspaper) that the shortages were a disguised blessing because overeating had formerly caused baldness among the Germans.[53] The shortages and substitutes must have had a radicalizing impact on common people because the burden of hunger fell so heavily on them and so lightly on the upper strata. Despite the profound crisis, class discrimination continued apace and the wealthy circumvented rationing by acquiring foodstuffs illegally.

In an equalitarian but empty gesture, everyone was subject to the same rationing. However, for those with money there was always food to be had on the black market that flouted price controls.[54] One young socialist woman described the reality of the rationing system for the average German:

Bread tickets were always insufficient for the many hungry mouths. Tickets were issued for meat you often could not get or had not the money to buy. Butter and fat tickets did not mean you could obtain the quantity indicated on them. More often than not the word "butter" on the ticket was all one saw of butter.[55]

There were many responses to this situation: silent despair, bitter complaining and often an increased hatred of the ruling classes. As noted, sometimes direct action in an attempt to get food led to riots. There was also clandestine organizing against the war at home and at the front. In a very public act of defiance, Socialist women gathered at the Bern International Women's Conference in March 1915. Held in neutral Switzerland, women came, often at great personal risk, from Germany, France, Great Britain, Czarist Russia, Poland, Italy, Holland and Switzerland. Neither the German nor French delegations were sanctioned by their parties, both of which followed an official policy of supporting their governments during the war.

Germany's Clara Zetkin, leader of the Socialist Women's Movement that had been part of the Socialist International, organized the meeting and drafted the final conference statement. This text was approved by an overwhelming vote of 21 to 6 with only the Russian followers of Lenin and a Polish delegate voting against. The final text in Zetkin's statement began:

> Women of the working people!
> Where are your husbands? Where are your sons?
> For eight months they have been at the front—torn from their work and their home. Youth, the support and hope of their parents; men in the prime of their life; men with graying hair, the providers for their families: clothed in uniforms, they all live in the trenches, under orders to destroy everything that diligent labor has created.
> Already, millions lie in mass graves. Many hundreds of thousands lie in the hospitals with shattered bodies, smashed limbs, sightless eyes, and broken minds, gripped by epidemics or prostrated by exhaustion.[56]

Nor were socialists the only women who organized European peace conferences in 1915. A much larger group gathered in The Hague from April 28 to May 1, 1915, to advocate two basic principles: (1) that conflicts should be resolved by peaceful means; and (2) that women should be given the right to vote. The Hague congress was attended by 1,300 women from 12 nations. These women formed the Women's International League for Peace and Freedom (WILPF) with Jane Addams, a Chicago social reformer, as their first President. In an attempt to promote their policies, 30 delegates toured Europe during May and June 1915 pleading their case to all who would listen.

Remarkably, there was even public anti-war protest within Imperial Germany despite the certainty of police repression. The last American Ambassador to Kaiser Wilhelm II's court, James W. Gerard, wrote of the ever-worsening morale among average Germans. Early in the summer of 1915, the first demonstration took place in Berlin: "About five hundred women collected in front of the Reichstag building. They were promptly suppressed by the police and no newspaper printed an account ... There was some talk of high prices for food, and the women all said that they wanted their men back from the trenches."[57]

Later, in November 1915, Frau von Blücher witnessed another such event in Germany's capital: "About 200 women trooped down the Linden, calling out 'Frieden, Frieden' (peace, peace) and at once 150 mounted police appeared on the scene with drawn swords to disperse the crowd." Although small in numbers the women's demonstration made an impact. One "common soldier on leave said that if the infantry at the front were to hear that their wives were being treated thus in their absence, whether they demanded butter or anything else, they would refuse to continue fighting."[58]

Women anti-war activists played a vital part in the distribution of illegal peace publications. Toni Sender tells of being summoned to the Frankfurt customs office to pay the required duty. Two large packages posted from Switzerland were brought out. Sender had a feeling that surely they must contain prohibited literature. She recalls her anxiety:

[An] officer unwrapped the parcels and out came dozens of books ... I was relieved when I saw on the paper cover the title *Das perfide Albion*, the slogan used against England by the German jingoes during the war. Rapidly the officer looked through the book.

"Seems to be good patriotic stuff," he said.

"Certainly, officer," was my answer.

Had he been a little more careful, however, he would have discovered under the paper cover the real title, *J'Accuse*, the famous book written by a German and accusing Germany, on the basis of authentic documents, of her share of war guilt.[59]

Had the official read more of the actual text, he would have arrested Sender at once.

As the fighting and dying continued, increasing disparity between war profiteering and mounting misery on the home front caused ever deeper alienation and radicalization. War production sustained very high profit levels for German corporations whose net earnings rose from 1,656,000,000 marks in 1912–13 to 2,213,000,000 marks in 1917. During the same years of suffering for the German masses, average dividends increased from 8.7 to 10.1 percent. Even these figures understate the wartime windfall accruing to German capitalists because, as one economist observes, "capital stock was watered down to avoid high nominal dividends and the dividend statistics do not do full justice to the actual profits that had been made."[60]

Rosa Luxemburg's terse epigram, "Dividends are rising—proletarians falling,"[61] forcefully captured the contradiction of an improving financial situation for German business in face of increased hardships for the average citizen. Taking note of the disparity between real wages and the cost of living confirms this observation (see Table 3.2).

Table 3.2   Index of real wages and the cost of living (1913 = 100)

Year	Real wages	Cost of living
1913	100	100
1914	93	103
1915	81	129
1916	74	170
1917	63	253
1918	64	313

Source: Based in tabulations from Ruhr miners' wage records in Gerald Bry, *Wages in Germany, 1871–1945*, Princeton, NJ: Princeton University Press, 1960: 322.

In 1914 and 1915, the situation was already unbearable: masses of soldiers died in the fighting, a countless number lost limbs, even more were blinded, and the death toll from disease and hunger was climbing higher as foot shortages carried on. But 1916 proved that things can always get worse with the horrific Battle of Verdun. Before the Battle of Verdun was over, 10 million shells were fired, equaling 1.35 million tons of steel within a 10 square mile area. This produced, literally, hundreds of millions of pounds of dead human flesh, resulting in the battle being called The Meat Grinder. France suffered 377,000 casualties as opposed to 337,000 for the Kaiser's army.[62] The other blood fest in 1916 was the battle of The Somme that pitted the Germans against mainly the British army. While Verdun was longer, The Somme was more deadly. Easily a billion pounds of dead human flesh was produced as the British and Allied forces reported 624,000 casualties while Germany had losses of 429,000.[63]

One of those to fall at the Somme was Eduard Offenbächer, a young student of political economy who had rallied to the Imperial German flag drunk on nationalism and a desire for adventure. Before he died, he wrote home expressing rather changed sentiments. A couple of weeks before his death, Offenbächer wrote, "What is the good of it all, considering that the ultimate result of the war was decided long ago? Is it in order to pander to the pride and thirst for glory of a few men who, through the influence of the Press, drive whole nations into the arena?"[64]

Yet, a large number continued to remain loyal to Kaiser and country. Take the case of monarchist seaman Richard Stumpf. As late as April 1916, Stumpf wrote in his diary proudly of his reputation as "patriotic" and denounced many of his shipmates as defeatists, complaining that the "only concern of this despicable rabble is their bellies."[65] However, with an increasingly critical stance against those above him, Stumpf wrote that he "would welcome the elimination of about two-thirds of our top-ranking officers," using as example one officer who the seaman claimed, "cleans and polishes his fingernails, combs his hair and only performs his duties when we are at sea."[66]

On May 1, 1916, on the Potsdamer Platz in Berlin, Karl Liebknecht was seized while attempting to address a May Day rally with about 2,000 participants, many members of the left socialist youth movement.[67] The demonstration called under the slogan "Bread! Freedom! Peace!" saw Liebknecht cry, "Down with the War! Down with the Government!" before he was taken into custody.[68] Liebknecht received a four-year sentence. Breaking up the anti-war rally in no way prevented the growth of anti-war sentiment, particularly within the socialist and labour movements. The SPD leaders could easily have taken a more critical stand and at least abstained during the vote for war credits. The reality was that in spite of "later claims, party leaders seem not to have been much interested in the mood of the working class."[69]

On December 15, 1916, twenty SPD deputies joined Liebknecht in voting against war credits and another twenty-two abstained. In January 1917, those who voted no were expelled from the SPD and in response, formed the Independent Social Democratic Party (USPD). It might have been possible to paint Liebknecht as a lone purist or crank before but now a significant portion of the working class's elected parliamentary representatives had expressed doubts if not opposition to the war. Notwithstanding their numerical minority, the failure of approximately 40 percent of the Socialist deputies to back the war unleashed controversy throughout the institutions of German labor. Furthermore, as *Vorwärts* noted, those opposed to the war actually represented more SPD voters than did the pro-war majority by a score of 1,380,590 to 1,372,058.[70]

What was the mood of the average soldier like by 1916? Leftist accounts assure us that many were ripe for revolt but then they would say that wouldn't they? It may be useful to turn to a middle-class and non-socialist eyewitness to verify these claims. Johannes Haas was middle class, and a devout Christian. At the start of his service, the two most pressing issues he wrote home about was his disgust with soldiers circulating pornography[71] and reflections on whether he should become a clergyman.[72]

By 1916, Haas is bitter about the "champagne and wine" officers who party while "*we* are dying in filth." Reporting on the mood of the average German soldier, he states the "only man who has any sympathy for or confidence in the Private Soldier is that ranter Liebknecht ... That and not the drivel of those who write dispatches, represents what the Field Greys really feel." He goes on to say, "I don't agree with the popular saying 'that there will only be peace when the bullets are aimed in the opposite direction,' but all the same there will be a fearful awakening some day!"[73] We will never know if he would have decided it best to aim the bullets "in the opposite direction." He was killed on June 1, 1916 at Verdun.

4

The Road to the
November Revolution

Death had become the constant companion for most Germans. Consider the stark statistics in Table 4.1, while remembering each number represents a human being with hopes, dreams, family and friends. Each of these people had been a part of a community that would never be the same again.

Table 4.1 German losses in World War I

Category	Number
Dead	1,808,000
Taken prisoner	618,000
Wounded	4,247,000
Disabled from war	1,537,000

Source: Rudolf Lindau, *Revolutionäre Kämpfe, 1918–1919*, Berlin: Dietz Verlag, 1960: 210.

These numbers, as horrific as they are, do not show the depth of pain felt by common German soldiers. Many left the battlefield physically intact but emotionally shattered. By 1918, at least one out of 20 beds in base hospitals had become reserved for what was termed "hysteria cases."[1] These poor men, who today would be diagnosed as having PTSD, received little sympathy from their largely conservative doctors. Most psychiatrists argued that "war, rather than being traumatic, is actually healthful and invigorating."[2] Unsurprisingly, many veterans disagreed with the good doctors' opinion.

At the end of the famous war novel *All Quiet on the Western Front*, the hero reflects on the fact that he is the last of his seven classmates left. Then he talks of the burning desire for peace throughout the army. "If there is not peace, there will be revolution," he concludes.[3] Such defeatism was not necessarily shared by the army high command.

In Dresden during May 1917, a female student from the United States recalled the hunger felt throughout the city. In what seemed like a dream she wandered into a place and was served elephant flesh: "The restaurant was packed as long as the elephant lasted."[4] The semi-starving Germans had slaughtered their prize zoo animals in despair. By 1917, for many of Germany's common people hunger, even outright starvation, was becoming increasingly and tragically commonplace. The number of civilian Germans who died as a result of the British naval blockade was massive; official figures report 763,000 deaths in World War I Germany were caused by the blockade. This figure does not include a further 150,000 Germans who died in the 1918 influenza pandemic to which they were more prone due to the malnutrition and related illnesses caused by the blockade.

Those most likely to die were the very young and the old. Most of all, the common people died; the poor citizens of Imperial Germany were unable to buy supplemental nourishment on the black market. Women not only lost husbands and lovers to death at the front, they also watched their children die due to the malnutrition (see Table 4.2).

In addition, the birth rate declined dramatically. The cause of this was not simply malnutrition and exhaustion. Many of the common people consciously chose not to have children. They had quickly grown, "pessimistic about the future, in which female children seemed destined to starve and male children destined for the mass grave." The longer the war groaned on, the more the people's "inner rejection of the conditions of war lent a political

cast to their desire to restrict the number of children they had."[5]
This was a birth strike, if you will.

Table 4.2   Index of child mortality (1913 = 100)

Sex	Age	1917	1918
Male	5–10	156.3	189.2
	10–15	154.3	215.0
Female	5–10	143.8	207.3
	10–15	152.9	239.0

Source: Rudolf Lindau, *Revolutionäre Kämpfe, 1918–1919*, Berlin: Dietz
Verlag, 1960: 209.

Any, let alone all, of the grim figures outlining the declining
welfare of the common people should have told the rulers in
Berlin that they were living on the edge of a volcano. Germany's
ruling class had previously been insightful enough to realize that
the only way to reduce emigration and temper political dissent
was through the introduction of massive social programs.[6] Now,
butter was sacrificed for guns and it would only be a matter of
time before the masses would no longer accept their situation.

Before the war was declared, there had been massive anti-war
demonstrations and rallies in German cities. The huge peace
protests in Berlin during July 1914 are most often cited in the
historical literature. After all, Berlin was the capital, where the
Reichstag (the German Congress) met, and widely considered the
most important city in Imperial Germany. It was not, however,
the only place in Germany where crowds had gathered against
war. These demonstrations took place despite the fact that the
moderate leaders of German Social Democracy had been hesitant
to rally the common people or even their own members against
the impending conflict. They repeated this hesitation many times
during the revolution with, if anything, more tragic results.

In many places, the SPD leadership was content with vague resolutions against the war and tried to leave matters to rest there. Still, like Berlin, local leaders in Leipzig, Solingen, Stuttgart, Düsseldorf and Kassel organized anti-war demonstrations. Seldom mentioned is the fact that in many other cities, the socialist rank and file "disobeyed their leaders and formed their own spontaneous demonstrations." Protesters were more often militant than passive as 6,000 clashed with police in Stuttgart while marching towards sites where pro-war rallies had been held. The confrontation became so violent, that the authorities called in the army.[7]

The role of repression has likewise been mainly underreported in historical narratives. Traditionally, historians have recounted that the police felt that they had to maintain order; these accounts reveal a one-sided interpretation of historical events. Police, the uniformed front line defenders of the existing order, were far from even handed when performing their duty. Somehow, they did not hesitate to attack, while on horseback and wielding swords, anti-war demonstrators as they overlooked groups singing patriotic songs.[8]

There were three areas of Germany where we have no evidence of any war enthusiasm in early 1914: "in the countryside, in the working-class areas of large cities, and in the areas near the border."[9] War enthusiasm was more commonly found among the wealthier members of society, sometimes likened to a drunken mob, even by the non-socialist press. *Tägliche Rundschau*, a nationalist newspaper, wrote that they regretted the "riot-like patriotism."[10] Even the Stuttgart Police Chief complained of certain people going crazy and seeing their neighbor as a French or Russian spy. Further, these civilians thought it their "duty to beat the spy and the policeman who protects the spy, until they are bloody, at the very least to make a big scene."[11]

War fever as promoted by the government at the beginning of the war, along with censorship and repression, silenced peace activists; it did not necessarily convert them. This should be born in mind when we examine overt acts of revolt in 1917. Popular pressure and ideological conviction drove many to form underground anti-war groups. These began as early as the outbreak of the world war. Some are rather well known like the group around Rosa Luxemburg, later called the *Spartaksubund*, or the Revolutionary Shop Stewards based largely in Berlin.[12] Most were local, often ad hoc organizations that at best make only a brief appearance on the historical stage, like Bremen's Left Radicals or the International Communists of Germany. Some are only known now through mention in survivor's memoirs, as is the case with the secret sailors group among members of the Imperial High Seas Fleet.[13]

Better known is how German Social Democracy splintered as an anti-war wing formed what became known as the Independent Socialist Democratic Party (USPD).[14] This splintering was more than a matter of personal "conscience" as some authors have argued. The fact is that the working class was against the war. They made this clear not with votes in parliament, but with strikes, quickly suppressed demonstrations and widespread anti-war propaganda. Working-class women were vital in all of these home front activities. Their male counterparts began to wonder if they had more in common with their officers or the workers in the enemy trenches, as shown by increased fraternization between soldiers wearing different uniforms.

All these factors began to come together by 1917. In Russia in 1917, two revolutions would fundamentally change that nation and the world. To the west in the French army, there would be a full-scale strike with soldiers refusing orders to attack. In Germany, society did not seem that unsettled. But appearances can be deceiving; 1917 is now understood to be the start of the German Revolution. Under the dark curtain of censorship and orchestrated patriotic pronouncements, the common people were stirring.

Käthe Kollwitz, a left-leaning artist, wrote on February 18, 1917 of attending a performance of the story of a waiter whose son falls "on the field of honor." Kollwitz describes how she "could scarcely keep control of myself, and I felt that I was not the only one." When the last word "Peace" is read, "someone in the audience called out aloud, as though overpowered by a tremendous emotion: 'Peace, Peace,' again and again ... there you have a peak behind the scenes. There you see the true feelings of people who to all appearances are bearing the war well."[15] Among those in loftier social positions there was a different kind of unease by 1917. Princess Evelyn Blücher wrote in her diary, one of the "strangest sign of the time is, to my thinking, the rapid and insidious way in which the tide of democracy is creeping on and overflooding all Europe."[16]

A case of "creeping democracy" might be seen in the April 1917 strikes that hit Berlin and some other urban areas. In Berlin, 200,000 workers struck for more food while raising some political demands after agitation by the Revolutionary Shop Stewards.[17] Partially at the urging of the *Spartaksubund* and individual radicals, 25,000 strikers continued the walkout asking not just for food but also stressing peace and democracy. At the same time, Leipzig saw 30,000 workers go on strike while Magdeburg and Kiel had 10,000 participants in each city. Unlike the initial Berlin walkout, the strikes in these three cities raised multiple political demands from the outset.[18]

These examples were not exceptional. The fact is that strikes, although illegal, increased throughout World War I (Table 4.3). By 1917 the number of striking workers surpassed peacetime figures and by the final year of the war the number was to double again. The quality of strikers' demands reflected the radicalization of the working class as did the political nature of the strikers' numbers. Moreover, a great many work stoppages directly challenged the state for its handling of food shortages, rationing, black marketeering, political repression and failure to end the war.[19]

Things were changing quickly within the German Navy as well. Sailors had been idle for most of the war, as the leaders of the High Seas Fleet knew it could not break through the British naval blockade. To make the situation more explosive, sailors were given far less in rations than fighting units of the army while still required to perform heavy physical labor. In addition, many came from strong pre-war union and radical traditions. By July 25, 1917, more than 5,000 sailors were members of an underground group with a central leadership called *Flottenzentrale*.

Table 4.3   Strikes in Germany during World War I

Time period	No. of strikes	Workers
January–July 1914	1199	94,014
August 1914	0	0
September–December 1914	24	1,126
1915	141	12,866
1916	240	124,866
1917	562	651,461
1918	773	1,304,248

Source: adapted from "Streiks und Aussperrungen 1914 bis 1918," in Jürgen Kuczynski, *Die Geschichte der Lage der Arbeiter Unter Dem Kapitalismus*, vol. IV, Berlin: Akademie Verlag, 1967: 249.

As the summer of 1917 went on, there were more and more incidents: hunger strikes as well as other forms of protest and minor acts of disobedience. On August 2, 1917, 400 sailors from *Prinz Regent Luitpold* mutinied and demanded an end to the war. The demonstration was quickly contained and 75 of the protesters arrested. Five leaders were tried, convicted and several executed by army firing squad.[20] Theodor Plivier, a sailor during the war and a participant in the later 1918 mutinies, wrote the novel *The Kaiser's Coolies*, which includes generous quotations from actual documentary records of these mutinies. Recreating the court martial, Plivier quotes the words of Alwin Köbis to the court, "We don't want annexations. We want a peace of understanding. And we'll get it. If need be, by all and every means … I admit openly that I did everything in my power to cripple the fleet by individual terrorism, so as to force a peace … We are social revolutionaries!"[21] Köbis, naturally, was one of the sailors executed by the firing squad.

Rather than realizing that this discontent was largely in response to the arbitrary and often brutal treatment sailors received at the hands of their officers, the Imperial Navy chose instead a simple and comforting explanation. That is, nothing was wrong with the way the Navy was run or how sailors were treated. All the dissent was merely the result of socialist propaganda and left-wing conspiracy. Thus, the Navy justified the harsh punishments they meted out.[22]

This violent repression on the part of the Imperial German Admiralty did not always eliminate dissent among the naval crews. On August 16, 1917, the stokers on the *Westfalen* went on strike because they did not get their customary extra rations for loading coal. The enraged sailors threatened the ship's Captain with violence. The leaders of this revolt were arrested based on evidence supplied by *agents provocateurs* disguised as sailors.[23] More long prison time and (suspended) death sentences followed.

Returning to the diaries of Seaman Richard Stumpf, which were highlighted in chapter three, one sees that his assessment of the sailors changed over time. No longer attacking fellow sailors as defeatists, he blamed the mutiny on the officers, "Manifestations of bitter anger due to the fact that the enlisted men are starving and suffering while the officers carouse and roll in money." Most of all, he blamed the Captain whose body he claimed was found floating in the submarine nets the morning after the mutiny was suppressed. "No one knows what happened … At any rate, it constitutes a warning to all officers."[24] Stumpf's diary entries no longer spit hate on England and he ridiculed the idea that foreign agents were behind the mutiny. All the same, he maintained his belief in the Kaiser's "pure intentions."[25]

It would be remiss not to mention the impact that the 1917 Russian Revolutions had on the common people of Germany. The first revolution in February/March removed the hated Czar from power while the second in October/November[26] took Russia out of the war. If the first revolution gave lie to the eternal nature of political structures, the second revolution ended any fears still remaining about Russians overrunning the German east. Further, the Bolsheviks, a group that proclaimed socialism as their goal, led the second revolution.[27] Therefore, there was a certain level of sympathy for Russia among wide sections of the German common people.

The Bolsheviks believed that their revolution could only survive if it spread to other war shattered nations of Europe. Most of all, they pinned their hopes on revolution in Germany and certainly not on the Kaiser's pure intentions. Despite their desperate need for peace, they delayed signing a treaty with Imperial Germany in the hope that a revolution would soon break out. Even when they finally accepted a separate and brutal peace treaty it was over the objections of much of the Bolshevik leadership.[28]

The way a victor's peace was imposed on Bolshevik Russia, basically at gun point, further alienated Germans who wanted a just peace. For many, the Russian Revolutions became an example of common people taking fate in their own hands. As one anti-war woman in Frankfurt asked, had not "the Russian shown an example to be followed?"[29] The Bolshevik government did everything they could to encourage this sort of thinking. In 1917 alone, the Russians clandestinely sent 60,000 leaflets into Germany. Also, several thousand copies of Lenin's *State and Revolution* were smuggled from Sweden and Switzerland into the Reich.[30] It is impossible to say how much, or what, impact the Bolshevik propaganda had. For Clara Zetkin, the most important thing about the Russian Revolution was not necessarily their brilliant political insights but the "mere fact that it occurred."[31]

Naturally, the Western Allies also aimed propaganda at the Germans.[32] Like the Bolshevik efforts, one can never determine the impact of this enterprise. Some have estimated that 40,000 to 50,000 German soldiers deserted to the Western armies, but there doesn't seem to be enough documentation to confirm accuracy of this estimate either way.[33] What scholars can confirm though is that Imperial Germany was concerned about propaganda efforts and desertion rates. As a German officer wrote on January 23, 1918, "There are people who would rather desert, who would rather hand themselves [over], than carry on another year." He noted that this feeling was even present among some officers.[34]

Still, as late as the fall of 1918, Field Marshal von Hindenburg could say that, "I did not consider that the time had come for us to despair of a successful conclusion of the war."[35] Likewise, military commander Erich Ludendorff, who later joined Adolf Hitler in his abortive 1923 putsch, continued to hold out hope of military triumph. If the Generals were stubborn and willing to go down fighting, the same could not be said of the large industrialists who were more flexible.

Even before the German Revolution had started in earnest, the old regime "was abandoned and practically buried alive by leading businessmen."[36] Carl Duisberg, the founder of *I.G. Farben* and later president of the Reich Association of Industry, was a case in point. Although he had been a solid defender of the war and Generals like Ludendorff late into 1918, by that same October Duisberg would tell a colleague that once he saw the present government "was bankrupt, I greeted the change to a parliamentary system with joy ... [I will support] the democratic government and, where it is possible, I work hand in hand with the unions ... You see, I am an opportunist and adjust to things as they are."[37] By the time of the revolution, Duisberg was convinced that the "red republic" was something he could not only survive but was an opportunity for profit as well.

By 1917, the German labor movement was hopelessly split. Those old SPD party leaders, whose feet were firmly planted in the soil of reformism and legality, could not abide the actions of the anti-war faction that challenged the status quo. This was more than a difference over supporting the war. For the leaders who pledged German Social Democracy to a class truce for the duration of the war, the masses were to be feared. The former thought the common people needed to be controlled by party and trade union structures lest they embark on foolish, "utopian," radical actions.

Whereas the moderates were anxious about the masses, the revolutionaries glorified the common people and thought them capable of great feats.[38] Therefore, they viewed the existing construction of society as a roadblock to the average Germans gaining control over their own lives and destiny. They were inspired by the thought of revolution. On the other hand, the old guard often agreed with SPD leader, Ebert when he said of social revolution, "I hate it like sin."[39]

As 1917 bled into 1918, there were many different camps among the common people of Germany. There was the old SPD and their affiliated trade unions; these still controlled most of the legal, formal structures of the labor movement. To their left, the USPD, or Independents, was a mixed bag of conflicting political ideologies united by their opposition to the war. The USPD would be the most broad and popular image of anti-war opposition by the last year of the war. Their ranks included Eduard Bernstein, the famous proponent of revisionism, Karl Kautsky, a theoretician once known as the "Pope of the European Socialism," and revolutionaries like Rosa Luxemburg and Karl Liebknecht.

The latter had been among the first to organize against the colossal blood bath known as World War I. Their group, that came to be known as the *Spartaksubund*, was relatively small and deprived of its most well-known leaders who were either serving jail sentences, drafted into the army, put into "protective custody," or even committed to mental hospitals.[40] Often overlooked by historians is that the work of the group continued because of the dedication of less known, largely female, militants.[41]

In addition to more traditional party organizational forms, there was the Revolutionary Shop Stewards, a group frequently neglected in discussions of Germany in war and revolution. Under the cover of official union meetings, opponents of the war discretely sought out likeminded delegates. To avoid the ever-present problem of police spies, the Revolutionary Shop Stewards network "started under the guise of a group of drinking buddies."[42]

Although they did not adopt the vanguard party model of the Bolsheviks, the stewards were extremely security conscious. Their organizational structure, while democratic among long-term, trusted union members, excluded workers who were new, temporary or could not be vouched for by an existing member.[43] Rather than full-time officials or rank and file members, most Revolutionary Shop Stewards like leader Richard Müller were section leaders whose work was voluntary and unpaid by the union.[44] Although Müller and many of his comrades advocated a system of council socialism[45] different from either Bolshevik centralism or traditional parliamentarianism, the Stewards' would suffer from what some say was the "lack of a coherent political vision."[46] To be fair, the same might be said with some justice about most other political formations.

If things were bad in Germany, they were worse in her ally, the Austro-Hungarian Empire. On January 14, 1918, the flour ration was cut by half and strikes broke out. At first, these were mainly outside Vienna but soon spread throughout the empire involving 700,000 workers and lasting ten days.[47] This put pressure on the war-weary Austro-Hungarian government, which was forced to feign agreement with the workers' peace program and otherwise concede to all their demands.

This example may have inspired radicals in Berlin, where worker representatives from major industries met on January 27, 1918. Acting on the proposal of Richard Müller, the conference resolved to call a general strike for the following day. The next morning, the lathe operators and Shop Stewards "signaled the beginning of the strike by striking the oxygen tanks used for welding with hammers. Within a few hours Berlin's entire armament industry came to a standstill."[48] The work stoppage had the participation of between 250,000[49] and 400,000[50] workers who elected delegates to formulate demands.

While the demands raised were not socialist in that the question of property was not even mentioned, they still illustrate the depth of anti-government feeling. Not content to make only economic demands, they asked for political change as in the call for: "The speedy bringing about of peace without annexations or indemnities, on the basis of the self-determination of peoples in accordance with the principles formulated by the Russian People's Commissioners in Brest-Litovsk."[51]

The strike embraced twenty-one major urban areas, and as before, the reaction of the military dictatorship was as swift as it was brutal. Long sentences were handed out freely by military courts which judged civilians accused of political crimes. On January 31, the general in charge of the Berlin District pronounced a state of siege. *Vörwarts* was forbidden and an attempt made by strikers to meet was dispersed by police. One SPD Reichstag deputy was given five years confinement in a fortress for attempting to address a strike rally in Treptower Park.

By February 3, with the workers exhausted and fearful of further repression, the strike had to be called off in Berlin, and workers in most other areas were likewise forced back to work.[52] The authorities made a dubious call by drafting Richard Müller and thousands upon thousands of like-minded dissidents into the army. Their oppositional activity continued within the German army, though strict military discipline moderated any immediate impact. But many of these reluctant warriors would be the yeast that helped inspire the rising of common soldiers in the months to come.[53]

Working people began to realize more and more the necessity of relying on their own strength. All through the spring and summer of 1918, German society disintegrated. The death agony of Wilhelmine rule was under way while a mass uprising was brewing. Workers became more radical and turned from their old leaders in favor of the USPD, the *Spartakusbund*, the Revolutionary Shop Stewards and other lesser radical groups. This trend was even more pronounced among younger Germans.[54] Still, many continued to yearn for the days of unity when the SPD represented most everyone on the left and was seen as the common people's vanguard.

The massive strikes in armament plants in January 1918 can be said to mark the active start of revolutionary upheaval. More than just about wages or conditions, the strikers demanded an end to the war and a peace treaty with Revolutionary Russia on the terms proposed by Leon Trotsky and the Bolsheviks. Then contemporary observers, and many subsequent historians, were quick to lay these strikes at the door of the usual suspects: the USPD or the *Spartakusbund*. It is now clear that the workers themselves effectuated these strikes through the agency of the Revolutionary Shop Stewards.[55]

The strikes were broken and the strike leaders were forcibly enlisted into the army; this move, however, only helped to further spread the flames of revolt. Throughout the year, there were increasing signs of the popular alienation from the war and the government. By October, it was a question of when rather than if a revolution would break out.

By 1918, numerous plots were hatched regarding a revolution. The USPD had cells plotting. The *Spartakusbund* considered the revolutionary possibilities while the Revolutionary Shop Stewards even set a date for the revolution. Radical groups, of all sizes and complexions were ready to give the signal for revolt.

As fate would have it, when the red flags signaling the outbreak of what has gone down in history as the November Revolution first appeared, they emanated not from workers in the factories, nor soldiers at the front. Not from the starving, rebellious people in the cities but rather from within the Imperial High Seas Fleet. Throughout the war, the spirit of Prussian militarism set the tone for relations between officers and men in the Imperial German Navy, which grew progressively more strained as time went on.[56]

The unwitting instigator of the revolution was Admiral von Trotha, the chief of staff of the High Seas Fleet. Admiral von Trotha, along with other high naval officers, dreamed up the rather unexpected idea of a full-scale attack by the German navy on the British fleet.[57] They hoped that by using the element of surprise, they might defeat the stronger British Royal Navy. On the other hand, as one Admiral remarked later, even "if the fleet had been destroyed, our proud, old Imperial Fleet with its officers and men would now be lying in immortal fame at the bottom of the sea instead of having been preserved in order to cover itself in cowardly fashion with disgrace ..."[58] Honor was extremely important to the gentlemen who ran the Imperial German navy. This appears to have been less a concern for the average sailor.

The sailors, if the reports sent to naval headquarters can be trusted, had taken to singing songs with lyrics like "we struggle not for Germany's honor, we struggle only for millionaires."[59] When the sailors got wind of what the Admirals were planning, they were not pleased.[60] Most thought that their Admirals were preparing for mass suicide.[61] "Rumors circulated to the effect that it had been decided to engage the enemy in a final encounter, in which the German fleet would triumph or die for the glory of the 'Kaiser and the Fatherland,'" one radical sailor recalled. He continued to explain, "The sailors of the Fleet had their own view on the 'Glory of the Fatherland'; when they met they saluted one another with a 'Long Live Liebknecht.'"[62]

Even if this radicalism was not universal, it is certainly indicative of the mood of large sections of the fleet's rank and file sailor. Thus, when ordered to sea, the crews on the *Thüringen* and *Helgoland* mutinied. From these ships the revolt spread to the *Markgraf* and the *Grosser Kurfurst*. In reaction, mass arrests were ordered, 151 sailors and 56 stokers on the *Thüringen* alone. This stabilized the situation in the short term but the disaffection was too strong to be easily suppressed.[63]

In a vain attempt to quarantine the mutinous element among the crews, Admiral Hipper decided to separate the squadrons of his battle fleet. Acting on the suggestion of Vice-Admiral Kraft, the third squadron was dispatched to Kiel against the advice of the naval commander-in-chief of that region.[64] No sooner had these ships docked when radical activity began anew. Petitions were circulated demanding the release of imprisoned comrades as the thin veneer of discipline began to crack; officers' orders went ignored with greater and greater frequency.

Demands that had been voiced were put into action when, on November 3, a crowd estimated at 20,000 moved on the detention barracks in the Feldstrasse. Street fighting broke out when the crowd encountered a line of armed sailors with orders to disperse the demonstration. Within minutes, nine people were killed and twenty-nine wounded. Reacting with horror, the men of the Kiel garrison realized the sailors could not turn back. Now that blood had been shed, they must continue their fight.

The same night, Karl Artelt, a USPD sailor, got the first sailors' council of the unfolding German Revolution elected.[65] By dawn, Artelt was head of a committee that represented 20,000 men. The shocked officers agreed to all the demands: abolishing of saluting, shorter periods of service, more leave, the release of those arrested. By nightfall, red flags floated over many a ship and sailors had arrested their most brutal officers.[66]

Despite promises by the authorities to the contrary, four infantry units were sent to surround, and most likely fire upon, the protesting sailors. Artelt and others got a car and drove out to meet them. The sailors explained the situation and demanded that they not fire on the sailors. The soldiers "like all of us simple workers and peasants forced into a soldiers' uniform without any actual relation to the war, joined our revolutionary movement. The officers were disarmed."[67]

When news of the events at Kiel reached Berlin, the shaken government now headed by Prince Max of Baden resolved to send a reliable but well-known Social Democrat to the port city to calm the revolutionary waters. The man chosen was Gustav Noske.[68] Noske, despite being a member of the SPD, was sympathetic to the right and Reich. Before Noske had an opportunity to use his powers of persuasion on the masses, a crowd mainly composed of sailors seized numerous buildings and set up a Sailors' and

Workers' Council. By November 5, Vice-Admiral Wilhelm Souchon, although no more guilty than a number of high officers was under arrest as red flags waved throughout Kiel.

Noske, an accomplished politician, quickly gauged the mood of the masses and was successful in maneuvering the majority of sailors and workers to his side. His success was so great that cheering crowds proclaimed him Governor of Kiel. In fact, he was even asked to be the first president of an independent Schleswig-Holstein to be created by leaving the Reich.[69] In any event, Noske promised to meet the most popular, pressing demands of Kiel—pardons, no troops brought in, no mutineers punished unless other crimes were committed—in exchange for a return to a more normal social and political climate at Kiel. The success of Noske in calming the revolutionary waters by a mixture of concessions, promises and appeals to the loyalty many commoners felt to German social democracy was to set a pattern of SPD maneuvers throughout the Revolution.

Meanwhile many sailors simply left. Some dedicated themselves to spreading the revolution. Others just wanted to go home. In either case, these seamen made government censorship ineffective as they brought the news of the revolution to city, town and village. Even those sailors who were more home sick than hell-bent on fanning the flames of rebellion, did not leave the same as they had first came. Richard Stumpf is a case in point. At the outbreak of the war, Stumpf had been Catholic, conservative, fiercely loyal to the Kaiser and the system he represented. On November 8, 1918, he confided to his diary the "unbelievable change" that had taken place within him. Within the past two days he had been converted "from a monarchist to a devout republican."[70]

All along the coastal area, the working people took the events at Kiel as the signal to rise up. News of the sailors' revolt in Kiel reached Hamburg on November 5 with an immense impact. Against the orders of their trade union leaders, a strike broke out in a shipyard. Soon the work stoppage had spread to all the yards. By early afternoon, harbor workers held a massive meeting and called for a general strike in support of the Kiel revolt and the abdication of the Kaiser.[71]

A hundred Wilhelmshaven mutineers, under guard to a prison camp, passed through Bremen where they were freed by popular crowds. The Workers' and Soldiers' Council was soon in command, with guards posted to ward off any government assault. By the end of the first week of November, not just Bremen and Hamburg, but Lubeck, Cuxhaven, Rensburg, Restock and other smaller towns were in the hands of the working class and other sections of common people.[72]

As the Empire that Otto von Bismarck had so carefully built was tottering under the blow struck from the north-west, the *coup de grace* was delivered by a revolutionary uprising in the kingdom of Bavaria.[73] Over one hundred thousand people assembled in Munich on November 7 to hear speeches demanding the Kaiser's abdication. After the rally broke up, revolutionary soldiers joined with the city garrison, and occupied all strategic points—railroads, telephone and telegraph offices, army headquarters and government agencies. Under the leadership of Kurt Eisner,[74] workers and soldiers elected delegates who took the Parliament building and used it for their deliberations. With the formation of a People's Republic of Bavaria[75] on November 8, the Bismarckian system was at an end. That even the conservative, Catholic Kingdom of Bavaria should succumb to revolution illustrated the depth of the German masses' radicalization. Now there would be radical change throughout the Reich, or Bavaria would make a separate peace with the Western powers.

With the fall of King Ludwig III and the Bavarian dynasty, any serious hope of containing the revolution vanished. By November 8, the major urban areas of Saxony, Baden, Hesse-Darmstadt, Wurttemberg[76] and the Thüringen states were all in open rebellion. The old semi-feudal states were powerless in the face of the determined action by workers, soldiers, sailors and citizens. One by one, old ruling dynasties were pushed off the stage of history by the rising tide of revolution. All these regional revolutions awaited word from Berlin that would mean the end of the Imperial Germany's political death agony and the proclamation of the long-awaited republic.

Wilhelm II may have been Kaiser by grace of God but by late 1918 he had been rejected by his own people. Big business deserted their Emperor and King while complaining that government incompetence had cost Germany the war.[77] The leaders of the armed forces forgot the warning of General von Falkenhayn in 1914 that suggested the victory was beyond Germany's reach. The generals, particularly Hindenburg and Ludendorff, needed a sacrificial lamb and his name was Kaiser Wilhelm II. Besides, the generals knew their soldiers would not fight to save Wilhelm's throne so they told him to abdicate. As one general told Prince Max of Baden, "Field-grey will not shoot at Field-grey."[78] That is, the soldiers of the Imperial Army were not willing to repress the radicals in uniform.

Kaiser Wilhelm II, by this time, cut a rather pathetic figure whose "actual influence on political decision-making was comparatively unimportant."[79] He had become a mere fig leaf for the rule of the generals and large industrialists who actually controlled the Reich. When his usefulness was over, the Kaiser was sacrificed by his most trusted field marshals in an attempt to save the Empire and, if possible, the monarchy. Sent into exile in the Netherlands on a night train like a tired Caesar in flight, this was the end of Imperial Germany. But the Kaiser left behind the generals, industrialists, autocrats, police and judges, the entire apparatus of his state.

5

The Kaiser Goes, the Generals Remain

The Kaiser fled. The war lost. At this point, many authors skip on to the founding of the German Republic in the eastern city of Weimar. Alternatively, they dive into US President Wilson's often-discussed 14 points for peace. If they linger long on the actual events of the German Revolution, it is frequently to bemoan the violence and the irrationality of the masses of common people. In reality, the violence of the German revolutionaries never came close to the levels seen in upheavals elsewhere. In spite of the tremendous joy felt by the average German, the revolution was not going to live up to its potential.

Throughout 1918, whether during the Naval revolt or the revolutions in places like Hamburg, Frankfurt, Bremen, Munich and Berlin, the radical left seldom used violence beyond a bare minimum. Many authors, particularly but not exclusively on the right, have exaggerated incidents of violence, accepted rumors as fact, and portrayed the crowds contesting control of the streets as debased mobs.[1] This anti-democratic attitude is based on ideological conviction not factual evidence. It is simply not useful, or honest, to conflate street protests with actual violence.

Erick Eyck, considered one of the most renowned historians of post-World War II Germany, is a case in point. When he discusses crowds at all he assigns to them a viciously right-wing character. For example, Eyck wrote:

[The] the murders of Karl Liebknecht and Rosa Luxemburg on January 16 [sic][2] created great excitement, but news of the death was welcomed by the great majority of Berliners as relief from a great danger; few asked themselves if justice had been done. But the victims' friends cried loudly that the two had been murdered by reactionary freebooters. And *today we can consider it established that at least Rosa Luxemburg was lynched by an excited mob.*[3]

Alternatively, radical authors typically simply point to the betrayals of mainstream Social Democracy and/or the lack of a Leninist party. The former head of the Red Army in Russia, Leon Trotsky distills all the complexity of the German Revolution to saying, the "thing lacking was a Bolshevik Party."[4] Matters were more complex than this. Of course, there is overwhelming evidence that the SPD leadership did betray their members, the common people and socialism. This chapter will illuminate that betrayal in more detail later. But it wasn't simply a matter of the revolutionaries needing a better organizational structure.[5]

Conditions in Russia and Germany were vastly different. Even Lenin recognized this, when in March 1918, during the Seventh Congress of the Russian Communist Party, he warned his listeners not to compare Western Europe with Russia. The Bolshevik leader warned that, "revolution cannot begin so easily in the advanced countries as the revolution began in Russia –in the land of Nicholas and Rasputin ... In such a country, it was as easy as lifting a feather ..."[6]

The three months from November 1918 through January 1919 were marked by confusion and conflict in Germany. A closer examination of these days may help reveal the logic and the contradictions of the revolutionary process. Let us turn first to events in the port city of Hamburg. On the morning of November 5, 1918, the city awoke to morning papers filled with the news of the sailors' mutiny in Kiel. Before mid-day, a strike completely unauthorized by the trade unions broke out in one of the shipyards. Within hours, harbor workers were calling for a general strike in support of the sailors and demanding the abdication of the Kaiser. The established labor movement was caught totally unprepared for these events and it was only with great effort that the mainstream

SPD was able to narrowly and inconsistently maintain control over the meeting held to discuss these ideas.

When the more radical USPD intervened later that day a list of demands was adopted, which included a general strike in support of socialist revolution. Interestingly, the big industrialists were, in some ways, prepared for this turn of events as they had been appealing to the Social Democratic trade unionists as early as October 1918. The richest and most powerful industrialists begged the SPD leadership to help fight "Bolshevism" in return for concessions that "no considerable body of German employers has ever granted before."[7]

At noon the next day, a crowd estimated to be 40,000 strong appeared on the streets in response to an USPD call. The meeting concluded with a demand for the proclamation of the Socialist Republic. Next, workers marched through the streets singing and chanting until a hail of gunfire hit the procession and killed a number of workers.[8] People demanded to elect Workers' and Soldiers' Councils, a practice that would be followed in many other cities and towns.

From November 7 to November 10, elections were held for the councils, which proved to be quite a challenge to the SPD plan to insist on a standard parliamentary government.[9] For the rest of 1918, struggles continued between radical and moderate sectors of labor. The SPD had a decided advantage in not actually putting forward much in the way of ideas or policies. Typically, the Hamburg SPD leaders limited themselves to proclaiming that their party was "the advocate of orderly processes and good government."[10] By 1919, they were able to dissolve the councils and continue down their self-anointed parliamentary road to socialism.[11]

The sailors' example impacted Frankfurt as well. Toni Sender, young USPD activist, shares her memory of convincing a non-commissioned officer to get the soldiers at the central railroad station to stop searching and detaining revolutionary soldiers and sailors travelling by train. By that same night, "two large red flags waved over the entrance of the Frankfurt central station."[12]

Whether speaking at the USPD meeting or chairing a shop stewards' meeting, Sender urged haste and argued against any idea that they should "wait for Berlin." The young woman warned rather prophetically that the revolution would be successful, "only if it succeeded in building up completely new administrations in the army, in government, and in the judiciary. It would not be enough that a high official or a judge placed a little red ribbon in his buttonhole."[13] Sadly, her words went largely unheeded. Rather, the old saying would prove true, "every policeman knows that though governments may change, the police remain."[14]

In Bremen, a party of radicals, calling themselves the International Socialists of Germany (ISD), had largely taken over the local SPD apparatus. This group, rebranded as the International Communists (IKD),[15] would later unite with the *Spartaksubund* and others to form the German Communist Party (KPD). The IKD built an extensive network of factory militants and had rapport with the local working class. When November 1918 came the people rose up just as the local radicals agitating for a council republic and the IKD joined the USPD to form a Bremen Red Guard of armed workers.[16]

Throughout Imperial Germany, revolution spread like proverbial wildfire ultimately winding its way towards Berlin, the capital. On November 6 there was fighting, that is some shooting and numerous fist fights resulting in the formation of a Workers' and Soldiers' Council in Düsseldorf. The same day workers marched with mutinous sailors in Halle and won over the soldiers of the 14th Regiment. Strikes on November 7 took place in Erfurt and a central council for the city was elected.[17]

In the southern German state of Bavaria, the Royal house of Wittelsbach was deposed on November 7 when hundreds of thousands marched into Munich demanding an end to the war and monarchy. Veteran radical socialist Kurt Eisner headed the march with a blind farmer named Ludwig Gandorfer who represented the Peasants' League. Workers' and Soldiers' Councils, which had sprung up like fresh grass after prolonged rain, established the "Bavarian Free State" with USPD member Eisner as the President.[18]

Chaotic meetings were held throughout the city hosting intense debates about the meaning of the Revolution. At one such gathering chaired by a woman, a Bavarian man in his thirties insisted on "the contributions made by women."[19] He insisted on people realizing that the revolution had only been possible because of the struggle of women. Although there were more than a fair number of intellectuals and artists who often had unrealistic or even silly ideas,[20] it would be wrong to think that the new government was initially without support from average people. A middle-class liberal whose politics were clearly not those of the radical left witnessed the events first hand and confirmed this popular support. Reflecting on one mass gathering, Victor Klemperer wrote, "this was truly a Bavarian people's assembly, quite obviously made up of workers, tradesmen, shopkeepers ... Where had this Munich enthusiasm come from?"[21]

Nor was this radical movement limited only to the Bavarian capital. The majority of the rural population had supported the revolution of November 7 and the leaders of the Peasants' League joined the USPD and SPD in the coalition government formed by Kurt Eisner. Peasant councils, rare elsewhere in Germany, touched 90 percent of farming communities by 1919. These organizations fought the great landowners and wished to divide up large estates so that farmers might own their own land. Their movement floundered between the rock of upper-class resistance and the indifference of many urban socialists. Yet later the failure of land reform led much of the rural population into apathy or even opposition to the revolution.[22]

The Revolution came to Leipzig on November 8, the day after it had come to Munich. After the red flag was raised in that Saxon city, the Revolution spread to Dresden and Chemnitz.[23] The Workers' and Soldiers' Councils that were established in different parts of Germany typically had different political compositions. Some were radical and led by the USPD such as in Halle where they "disarmed the police and vested its own security organs with responsibility for ensuring order."[24] Some were more timid like the Essen Workers' and Soldiers Council that quickly became co-opted into the existing administration.

Not surprisingly, women were active in all these movements. Working-class women, "were the first to express criticism of the war and they did so most emphatically."[25] In many actions, small and large, women had laid the groundwork for the German Revolution. Whether by peaceful peace protests or disorderly bread riots, it had been women who consistently raised the anti-war temperature of the people. The Weimar Republic would later reduce the radical activity and involvement of women.[26] That is not to say, that individual female activists—like Clara Zetkin, Toni Sender, Rosa Luxemburg, Käte Duncker, Mathilde Jacob, Fanny Jezierska, and Berta Thalheimer or, in the world of art, Käthe Kollwitz—did not continue to make their mark.

Nor were female revolutionaries the unfeeling barbarians of rightist mythology. Women leftists were portrayed as savage and uncaring, like bloody "Red Rosa". Women were blamed for the revolution and the image of wild, feminized crowds led to a "profound crisis of gender identities."[27] As one scholar discovered, "the cultural imagery of the brutalized feminized mob was a crucial component of the mobilization of society to accept violence against the 'internal enemy.'"[28] In truth, they may have been radicals, but women activists were also mothers, wives, friends, neighbors and lovers.

The idealism and passion they possessed is typified in a letter that Käte Duncker wrote to her son Karl as the first light of the revolution was breaking through the dark clouds of government censorship. It is worth citing at length:

Käte to Karl Duncker
Steglitz, 3 November 1918

My dearest boy!

The next few weeks will probably be moving wildly, no one can know what they bring us. We who have long fought for a new, better time with words and writing, cannot remain in the background, we must fight. My boy, who is far from us, but you have to understand. Now the ground is plowed to its depths by four years of world war, now or never must the seed of socialism be dispersed.

Now or never, the small but powerful group of people who in every country uses the immense majority of the population only as a material for their purposes, as workers, as soldiers, as taxpayers etc., must be removed. Now or never, we must try to make available all the goods of culture and technology to all humanity, which until now only one small minority has had access to ... Certainly, there will be differences in the future, but only the differences of personal endowment, no more the differences of money and education ...[29]

What was happening in Berlin? In the old capital of the Prussian kings, the land of Frederick the Great, former home of Kaiser Wilhelm II, the leadership of the SPD was moving heaven and earth in an attempt to maintain some semblance of the old system, the very system which was being so powerfully rejected by the masses in city after city. Following the lead of Friedrich Ebert, the Social Democratic leadership worked on increasing their influence in the liberal monarchical government of Prince Max of Baden. Ebert and his close associates not only refused to consider any radical alternatives, but sought to derail the speeding train of revolution.[30] This was no small task since, like Prince Max or key army leader, General Groener, who worried about control of the armed forces, Ebert was fearful of losing command of his own political party.

In a flyer widely circulated on November 4, an increasingly worried Social Democratic leadership attempted to mobilize their supporters for inaction. It reads in part:

> Through anonymous flyers and by agitation from mouth to mouth you have been asked in the next days to leave your work and go onto the streets. We ask you not to follow this advice ... Rash acts may bring horrible disaster to the individual and to our party. Action that promises success must have the support of the entire body of the working class. Yet for this action the moment is not ripe.[31]

Reports from SPD activists back to the party headquarters suggested that this and other efforts were having a limited effect. It became crystal clear that something had to be done to at least give the appearance of change.

While bitter over their ultimate failure to save the Imperial throne, the Kaiser appreciated the support he received from the leaders of German Social Democracy. In his *Memoirs*, the deposed monarch comments he was "well aware that many who rally around the Social Democratic banner did not wish revolution; some of the individual Social Democratic leaders likewise did not wish it at that time, and more than one among them was ready to co-operate with me."[32] Unfortunately for the second and last German Kaiser, he was already yesterday's man long before November 1918.

After all, someone had to be blamed for all the death and suffering. What was needed was a scapegoat, and Kaiser Wilhelm II would do nicely. Thus, the loyal working-class advocates of the SPD Executive demanded the Kaiser's abdication on Wednesday, November 6, in a meeting at the Reich Chancellery with Prince Max and General Groener. While Groener still balked at the idea, Prince Max made arrangements to discuss the matter further with SPD leader Ebert the following morning.

The Kaiser's last Imperial Chancellor later recorded the decisive portions of his conversation with Ebert. What Prince Max desperately wanted to know was whether the Social Democrats could be counted on to fight the revolutionary movement if Kaiser Wilhelm II abdicated. Ebert, the future President of the Weimar Republic, told Prince Max that, "*After* the Kaiser's abdication he hoped to bring round party and masses to the side of the government."[33]

Once the Kaiser had his valets packed for his flight to Holland and the Crown Prince had given up his claim to the throne, Prince Max established regency and appointed conservative Social Democrat Ebert as Imperial Chancellor. Both men hoped to somehow save the institution of monarchy. They wanted a reformed and very constitutional monarchy to be sure, but a monarchy all the same. It was like dancing in the dark as the few who cared about constitutional legality questioned whether one Chancellor could appoint another. But most commoners of the Reich didn't care about these fine points of constitutional law.

On the early afternoon of November 9, 1918, "large crowds of workers and soldiers poured into the city center to celebrate the news of the Kaiser's abdication."[34] Increasingly, shouts of "Long Live the Socialist Republic!" echoed through the air. As the day went on the size of the crowds grew. One non-socialist Reichstag deputy, Hans Hanssen, witnessed the images of that time and recorded his perceptions in his memoirs. Around noon, Hanssen was returning to the Reichstag from a restaurant on Potsdammer Plaza. He saw throngs of people on the streets in larger and larger numbers while "red flags, revolutionary songs, and shouts for the Social Republic were seen and heard everywhere ... [at the Reichstag building were] a score of fully equipped riflemen and above them a huge red flag. Sailors with cartridge belts across their shoulders and rifles in their hands stepped forward, ready for battle."[35]

A group of workers and soldiers approached SPD leader Philipp Scheidemann in the dining hall of the Reichstag building and begged that he speak. "I refused," he recalled, "how many times had I already spoken!" But the requests continued, "You must, you must [speak], if trouble is to be avoided. There are thousands upon thousands outside shouting for you to speak. Come along, quick, Scheidemann! Liebknecht is already speaking from the balcony of the Schloss."[36]

The last moved Scheidemann to action. Realizing the mood of the masses and Liebknecht's effectiveness as a speaker, he moved to forestall what he perceived as "Bolshevist tyranny, the substitute for the tyranny of the Czars." Scheidemann not only spoke; he announced the formation of the German republic and of a labor government to lead it. Since all socialist parties were invited to participate in the government, the proposal effectively undercut revolutionary agitation, at least in the short run.

Scheidemann's impromptu proclamation did not reflect the considered decision of German Social Democracy or her allies. Indeed, his fellow social democrat, Friedrich Ebert, was at first outraged at Scheidemann's behavior. Ebert's face turned livid with wrath as he lectured to Scheidemann: "You have no right to proclaim the Republic."[37] As time passed, and the depth of popular discontent was increasingly appreciated, proclaiming the republic came to be regarded as a stroke of genius by those wishing to preserve some form of bourgeois rule in Germany.[38]

Another maneuver of equal importance was the SPD's invitation to the USPD leadership to participate in the government even if they chose to nominate Karl Liebknecht as one of their ministers. This ploy stimulated discord within the USPD ranks, as the party divided on the SPD proposal.[39] While USPD leftists were doubtful of cooperating with the same party that had supported the war, the right-wing wanted to go home to the SPD with all the bloodshed forgiven. Eduard Bernstein, who had tangled with Rosa Luxemburg over his support for reformism as opposed to her advocacy of revolution, confided his belief in unity with the SPD "even if we have to break with the Left. Scheidemann and his people are at present pursuing the only right policy."[40]

This was a day when downtown Berlin was full of all sorts of political activity and not just by the rich and the famous men of the dying Empire. The common people who had endured so much in the last four years of war and hunger surged through the streets. They appeared chaotic but there was logic to their activities, whether defacing symbols of old Imperial Germany or shouting out their desire for a social republic. They thought the day of the people had arrived. The crowd of commoners intruding into the public space, formerly reserved for the control by the rich and rulers, was intolerable to guardians of the status quo. Although the crowd was largely peaceful and attacked mainly symbols of the old order rather than people, they had to be muscled out of the picture.[41]

Even if the crowds in November bore scant resemblance to the images of those in the French Revolution's reign of terror, they terrified the ruling class all the same. One noblewoman spoke to her diary of her fear of going out as "there is a seething mass of people constantly coming and going. Sinister-looking red flags are waving ..."[42] Princess Blücher wrote of her anxiety over "strange-looking loafers hanging about the street." Yet her real surprise was reserved for witnessing "the pale gold of your girls' uncovered heads, as they passed by with only a shawl over their shoulders. It seemed so feminine and incongruous, under the folds of those gruesome red banners flying over them. One can never imagine these pale northern women helping to build up barricades and screaming and raging for blood."[43]

The Princess's diary gives a far more honest, even if at times inaccurate, portrait of the revolutionary crowds than the nightmarish fantasies conjured up by those on the militaristic right-wing.[44] Major Gustav Böhm, an official in the Prussian Ministry of War, reduced all the nuances and variety of the revolutionary crowds down to an evil conspiracy. Böhm warned that Karl Liebknecht was "collecting an evil mob of criminals and deserters around his flag, he is supposed to be paying them 20 marks a day. The money is obviously coming from Russia. An organization for the elimination of officers has been created."[45]

Further, it is important to remember that the actors in this drama of revolution were not just men. Women were an essential component of the revolution. They were transformed by the revolution in both self-image and their representation in society. Now, women were seen, and saw themselves, as more forthright, independent if not uncontrollable figures after war and revolution. Historian Kathleen Canning has even argued that the German Revolution caused a "shattering of the gender order."[46] No matter what one thinks of this argument, it is certain that women could no longer be simply dismissed as camp followers of the men in their life.

For example, Käte Duncker had been in the inner city on the morning of November 9. She had proceeded to Moabit,[47] where, with the help of armed workers and soldiers she freed fellow radicals imprisoned in that detention center. That evening, Lotte Pulewka recalled how she joined her Spartaksubund comrades in a building on Wilhelmstrasse that evening. Among those present were Käte and Hermann Duncker, Karl Liebknecht, Leo Jogiches and many others. This heavily female gathering proceeded to have a sophisticated political discussion of strategy and tactics.[48]

On the following evening, Mathilde Jacob directed them to the editorial office of the *Lokal-Anzeiger*, which was turned into the *Rote Fahne* (Red Flag). Everything was in flux:

> The submissiveness with which the gentlemen and all the staff on November 9 had pretended to be subject to the revolutionary will of the proletariat had given way to an increasing sabotage and resistance. The gentlemen of the publishing house and the editors now rushed to the government and screamed at the wicked robbery of their property.[49]

The new "socialist" government ordered the papers to be returned to their former owners. By November 11, the revolutionaries had to abandon this short-lived outpost of far-left agitation.

A curious incident illustrates the confusion that accompanied the November Revolution. A group of revolutionary soldiers found themselves in possession of a truckload of banknotes. They decided to hand these over to, what they saw as, the revolution. So, the soldiers dumped a mountain of money onto the floors of the USPD's caucus room. The USPD leaders had no idea what to do with this windfall and finally meekly returned it to the *Reichsbank*.

They later regretted their actions and wished they had retained the currency for use by revolutionaries. As one historian has remarked, "this episode shows how the revolutionaries of November 9 underestimated the staying power of the state apparatus. It was a misunderstanding that would contribute to the failure of the Revolution."[50] In handing back to the *Reichsbank* this forest of paper wealth, the revolutionaries had shown their honesty but not their wisdom.

The issue of power arose when the Workers' and Soldiers' Councils allowed a six man Council of People's Deputies to be formed on November 10.[51] This, the first decisive battle between the forces of moderation and those of revolution within the peoples' movement took on the question of who would govern: democratically controlled councils or a traditional parliamentary government.[52]

The Councils, which were by their very nature revolutionary institutions, could not co-exist with the conventional, bourgeois political structures that the SPD bureaucrats intended to create. The institutional muscle of German Social Democracy proved more powerful than revolutionary idealism; the majority of delegates elected to the Workers' and Soldiers' Councils were either members or supporters of the SPD.[53]

In such a situation, conflict was inevitable and could not be long forestalled. It was the belief of the revolutionary left that the council movement was inherently an attack on capitalism regardless of its momentary moderate makeup. As people radicalized, the Councils might have become the natural vehicle for this sentiment and this might quickly change the political outlook of these institutions. This democratic faith in the working masses contrasts sharply with frantic efforts of the right-wing SPD leaders to usurp the power of the movement.

In addition, the government proposed by the SPD was to be one that would not interfere with the property rights of the great industrialists and landowners. When the Executive Committee of the Councils became paralyzed, the Council of People's Deputies took over more and more power. On November 23, the Executive Committee officially conceded power to the Council of People's Deputies.[54] With the decision to hold elections for a National Assembly, the Council Movement was effectively finished.[55]

Rosa Luxemburg sarcastically commented: "What is the program of the new government? It proposes the election of a President, who is to have a position intermediate between that of the King of England and that of the President of the United States. He is to be, as it were, King Ebert."[56] This development was not merely a reflection of the situation in Berlin, nor was its opposition limited only to Rosa Luxemburg and the far left.

In Frankfurt, Toni Sender recalled how conservatives of all shades were suddenly frantic to hold elections to the Constituent Assembly. Although they had shown little interest in democracy for 60 years, the right now clamored, "No delay of general elections!"[57] Unlike those further to her left, Sender was no opponent of a parliamentary government *per se*. However, she argued in the Frankfurt Workers' Council that such an election needed to be delayed.

Among her reasoning was that soldiers were just returning after years of military censorship and were still preoccupied with keeping themselves alive. She explained that they needed time to update themselves on the political situation and reflect on the meaning of the Revolution. Further, to "satisfy the claims of the revolutionary masses" a fundamental change in Germany's political and economic structure was needed. That is, to "dethrone those powers responsible for the past."[58] The right-wing Social Democrats, on the other hand, desired elections because they "were not prepared for revolutionary changes and were perfectly satisfied to have only parliamentary government."[59]

Sender did not foresee a fatal problem. That was, the old SPD leaders were almost as terrified by the crowds in German city streets as the old ruling class. Rather than turning to the common people or their own party members to form a new republican army, they fought against the revolution by turning first to the Imperial Army and then to *Freikorps.*[60] An alliance was begun with the legendary telephone call of November 10 from the Prussian General Groener to Ebert, the Social Democratic leader.

Exactly what was said has been hotly debated, but the general's later statements indicate that the charges of a pact being made against the revolutionary working-class movement are well taken. The fictional account in Plivier's *The Kaiser Goes: The Generals Remain* captures the spirit, if perhaps not the letter, of this conversation:

A telephone rings in the Chancellery. The President of the Social Democratic Party has the receiver in his hand:

"Ebert speaking."

"Groener speaking."

Quartermaster-General Groener has consulted his staff and discussed the matter with Field-Marshal von Hindenburg. The army asks the support of the Social Democratic Party for the restoration of its lost authority. As a price, the Generals offer to the new Government the protection of their bayonets and guns.

Chancellor Ebert listens attentively to the First Quartermaster General Groener's proposals. Then he asks:

"What is your attitude toward the Workers' and Soldiers' Councils?"

"Commanders have been instructed to deal with them in a friendly spirit."

"And what do you expect of us?"

"The General Field-Marshal expects the Government of the Reich to support the Officers' Corps in the maintenance of discipline and order in the army. He asks also that the provisioning of the army shall be ensured by every possible means and that any disturbance of railway communications shall be prevented."

"Anything else?"

"The Officers' Corps invites the Government of the Reich to fight Bolshevism, and for this purpose places itself at the Government's disposal."

Ebert hesitates before giving his answer. He looks up at the thickly padded door; he turns toward the window and listens for any sound from the street, where he fancies he already hears the enraged shout of the workers.

Then in a confident voice he replies:

"Convey to the General Field Marshal the thanks of the Government."[61]

Regardless of any inaccuracies this version may contain, it was based on the facts as told by General Groener. The significance of this SPD-Army pact should not be underestimated. This pact was ongoing as Social Democrat Ebert talked to militarist Groener via a secret telephone line. One historian notes, "Each night between eleven and one, the two men in whose hands the destiny of Germany rested talked together without fear of being overheard and, in Groener's words, 'reviewed the situation from day to day according to developments'."[62]

This Faust-like deal was to allow the Army high command to survive. A little over a decade later, the Army high command would then turn power over to the Nazis. It was, also, an arrangement that the old leaders of the Imperial German Army were ill-equipped to fulfill even in the first months. Philipp Scheidemann recalled later, "The commanders of the troops that first arrived took the oath of loyalty and obedience for themselves and their troops ...

Nothing came of it. The soldiers vanished overnight completely; they would not stop; they wanted to go home."[63] It is estimated that of the nine or ten divisions sent from the front lines to aid the government, only something like 800[64] to 1400 men remained by December 11, 1918.[65]

At the time, Berlin was the headquarters of the People's Naval Division. This group was composed at its core of several hundred sailors who had come from Kiel during the early stage of the revolution. The People's Naval Division was seen as the Revolution's military elite. The Division had been installed in the Imperial Castle and nearby royal stables on November 15. This strategic position was something that the provisional government felt unable to tolerate.

After a long series of negotiations in December, the sailors agreed to vacate the Castle and reduce their force to 600 men. For this concession, the government was to provide a Christmas bonus of 80,000 marks. Then, in what has all the markings of a provocation, the government went back on the promised payment. On December 23, the People's Naval Division reacted with anger and seized Otto Wels, the Commandant of Berlin, along with two other leading Social Democrats.

Further, the sailors occupied the Chancellery along with the central telephone and telegraph offices. With Ebert under virtual house arrest in the Chancellor's palace, the sailors were confident that their view of justice would prevail in the matter. Unknown to them was the existence of a secret and direct line between Ebert's office and the Supreme Command. The same day, regular troops entered central Berlin to free Wels and "finish once and for all the People's Naval Division."[66]

Although these troops commanded by General von Lequis had some initial success, the sailors were reinforced by armed workers, a group calling itself the Republican Soldiers' Army and units of police chief Emil Eichhorn's Security Force. Once it became obvious that the sailors would not be easily dislodged, the regular troops were forced to retreat. In despair, Major von Harbou told

Army headquarters: "Troops of the General Command Lequis can no longer be used in action. I see no way of protecting the Government with the means so far employed."[67] This news led military leaders to speed up their organization of *Freikorps* units to fight against what they perceived as anarchy.[68]

The triumph of the People's Naval Division proved to be more apparent than real. While the government was forced to give in on the issue of the Christmas bonus, later negotiations led to the destruction of the sailors as a political force, as they were maneuvered into accepting the jurisdiction of the City Commandant over their unit. In addition, the sailors pledged to take no further action against the government. Nonetheless, the episode *Rote Fahne* labelled "Ebert's Bloody Christmas"[69] had a deep impact upon the revolutionary process.

Most immediately, the attack on the People's Naval Division with its resulting loss of life put the USPD leadership in an untenable position. The three Independent Social Democrats in the government had not been consulted in the matter and, not surprisingly, were furious to discover that unlimited authority had been granted to the Minister of War to repress the sailors. Unable to map a strategy that would allow them to utilize their positions to curb the SPD, USPD members Haase, Dittmann and Barth resigned from the Council of People's Commissars, leaving the uppermost reaches of the governmental structure completely in the hands of Social Democrat Ebert and his circle.

By December 29, the ruling council began to refer to itself as the Reich government, jettisoning the more radical title employed when the three USPD members were around. Of no real significance in and of itself, this change in language speaks of the way in which the SPD leaders envisioned the new Germany. Of greater import was the withdrawal by the USPD of their people from almost all leading positions within both the national and Prussian governments.

As the Independents retreated in revulsion at the SPD collaboration with the military establishment, Berlin's populace grew ever more alienated and bitter. To many it seemed as though the revolution was being stolen from them, and that their erstwhile leaders had betrayed them. This mood was captured on December 29 at the funeral procession for the sailors killed during the holiday fighting. Thousands marched chanting, "Down with the traitors!" as numerous posters read, "Who killed the sailors? Name them we can: Ebert, Landsberg and Scheidemann."[70]

This would lead the SPD leaders to make another mistake,[71] one that proved fatal for the Revolution and also prepared for the overthrow of the Weimar Republic. Their fear of the revolutionary crowds and their far left opponents was so great that they next turned to the *Freikorps*, those paramilitary groups that drew heavily from the old Imperial officer corps. It is true the *Freikorps* hated revolutionary crowds and the far left, but they hated parliamentary democracy with almost the same passion.

6

Provocation, Revolt and Repression

Imagine ordinary Germans living through the chaos, insecurity and uncertainty brought on by war and popular upheaval. The November Revolution instilled in many hope for a better future yet this optimism had to compete with day-to-day doubts and fears. Now, envision facing this complicated situation while hungry and worried about the source of your next meal. It is often forgotten that the signing of an armistice in November 1918 did little to ease the food crisis.

Food was a weapon and a stick held over the head of Germany until finally lifted in July 1919, the better part of a year after the last shot of the war was fired.[1] Women in Frankfurt had sent a radio message to the United States begging for an end to the blockade. The blockade went on. No surprise that many felt like Toni Sender did when she expressed that the Allies' conscious prolonging of hunger appeared to be "directed exclusively against the civil population, starving women and babies."[2] In truth, it was designed to preempt any radical second revolution.[3] When in late 1918, revolutionary Russia offered to send two trainloads of grain, the proposal was rejected because it would have precluded a much larger amount of food promised by the USA. Unfortunately, the American relief was not to arrive for another four months.[4]

Keeping the defeated Germans in a state of hunger if not semi-starvation was also supposed to destroy German militarism. While it might be argued that the goal of preventing radical revolution was a success, the shortage of food fed the power of the militarists. With limited food sources, reactionary militarists acting through the army or the *Freikorps* were able to manipulate supplies for entire towns. Thus, the blockade strategy, far from reducing German militarism, "in practice very quickly nourished its regeneration in a civil war against the soldiers' and workers' Councils that cost 15,000 lives in the first nine months of 1919."[5]

In addition, the split between urban and rural populations was aggravated by the ongoing blockade. In 1919, resistance by farmers to forced cattle sales was so fierce that the army created special twenty-man units to help officials gather livestock. In Westphalia, government inspectors "were greeted by peasants armed with clubs and pitchforks threatening to kill the intruders."[6] The association of "socialism" with a government that requisitioned food caused the growth of rightist sentiments in many a peasant's mind.

Not that life was so great in the cities and towns. In addition to the lack of food, there was a lack of employment (see Table 6.1). The economic misery that had engulfed the working class was particularly acute in Berlin and pushed caution aside in many proletarian minds. During the period preceding the January crisis, the number of unemployed rose dramatically.

Table 6.1   Unemployed relief recipients, 1918–1919

Date	Number
December 1, 1918	501,610
January 1, 1919	905,137
February 1, 1919	1,076,368
March 1, 1919	1,053,854
April 1, 1919	829,758
May 1, 1919	700,000
June 1, 1919	620,000
August 1, 1919	550,000

Source: Jürgen Kuczynski, *Die Geschichte der Lage der Arbeiter Unter Dem Kapitalismus*, vol. V, Berlin: Akademie Verlag, 1966: 159

The founding of the German Communist Party (KPD) at the end of 1918[7] increased tension as the masses were provided potential revolutionary leadership and the Social Democrats potential scapegoats. Within the Berlin working class, nerves grew strained and tempers began to flare. Finally, this social tinderbox was sparked by the dismissal of USPD member Emil Eichhorn as Berlin chief of police by SPD Prussian Prime Minister Paul Hirsch.[8] Many radicals viewed this as an attack on the gains of the revolution by the Social Democratic government. On January 5, protests and demonstrations started in Berlin. These protests grew in strength before devolving into street fighting that lasted until January 13.

From the government point of view, Eichhorn was irresponsible, even dangerous, as he openly sided with the revolutionary left. The fact that he armed 1,500 workers who proceeded to fight on the side of the rebellious People's Naval Division did little to win him the respect of conservative opinion. To lay the groundwork for his dismissal, public opinion was molded through a widespread and vicious campaign of libel, utilizing the pages of bourgeois and Social Democratic newspapers. On January 3, 1919, Eichhorn was summoned to the Prussian minister of the interior to answer a series of accusations. Although he pledged to submit a detailed written response to the charges, Eichhorn received his dismissal order the next day.[9]

Upon receipt of this document, Eichhorn went to the offices of the Berlin USPD. A routine meeting with the Revolutionary Shop Stewards was scheduled for that evening, but as a result of this new development a mass protest meeting was called for Sunday, January 5. Once notified, the Central Committee of the KPD agreed to join this demonstration provided the response be limited to protest. Soon the streets of Germany's capital were flooded with flyers issued in the name of all three organizations. The text read, in part:

"Attention! Workers! Party Comrades!
    The Ebert-Scheidemann government has heightened its counter-revolutionary activities with a new *contemptible*

conspiracy directed against the revolutionary workers of Greater Berlin: it tried *maliciously to oust Chief of Police Eichhorn from his office.* It wished to replace Eichhorn with its willing tool, the Prussian minister of Police, Ernst.

By this action, the Ebert-Scheidemann government wishes not only to remove the last trusted man of the revolutionary Berlin workers, but primarily it intends to *establish a despotic rule antagonistic to the revolutionary workers.*

Workers! Party Comrades! The person of Eichhorn is not the main issue; you yourselves will lose the last remnants of your revolutionary achievements through this major blow ...

Workers! Party Comrades! *This you cannot and must not permit!* Therefore, turn out for powerful *mass demonstrations.* Prove your power to the autocrats of today; prove that the revolutionary spirit of the November days has not been extinguished.

Come today, Sunday, at 2 p.m. to the impressive mass demonstrations in the Siegesallee! ...

Long live revolutionary, international socialism!

Berlin, January 5, 1919.

Revolutionary Shop Stewards and Representatives of the large factories of Greater Berlin.

Central Committee of Greater Berlin Social Democratic Election Association of the Independent Social Democratic Party.

Central Committee of the Communist Party of Germany (Spartacist League).[10]

The leaders who wrote this joint call did not expect a good turnout, not on a Sunday. Berlin's common people were more incensed than the party intellectuals realized. Some radicals, including many metal workers in Berlin, believed the second revolution was at hand. Confusion was rampant throughout the society and the upper classes, and many right-wing Social Democrats feared a Bolshevik-style revolution. An unexpectedly large number of people turned out for the Sunday protest and another was set for the next day.

> On Monday, January 6, central Berlin saw one of the most powerful mass demonstrations of the city's workers of this period, with around 200,000 demonstrators on the streets. The revolutionaries in Berlin had achieved a great triumph and it seemed that the Ebert–Scheidemann government might fall in the face of this sizeable opposition. However, the "Revolutionary Committee" was incapable of taking action. The leading members were preoccupied with delivering speeches to the demonstrators, and, above all, with trying to win the Berlin troops into supporting the revolutionary left ...[11]

A USPD workers' council member Stahlberg, took part in the demonstration and a few days later gave this report: "The masses called for the leaders to give them directions for further actions, but the leaders were not [at] hand ... It was total confusion."[12] Berliners were ready to do something but even the far-left leaders weren't prepared to signal what that would be. As another participant later recounted:

> What happened on Monday in Berlin was perhaps the greatest proletariat mass action in history. We do believe that not even in Russia were there mass demonstrations of this size. From Roland to Viktoria, proletarians were standing shoulder to shoulder. Deep into the Tiergarten they were standing. They had brought along their weapons, they had their red flags. They were ready to do anything, to give everything, even their lives. There was an army of 200,000 such as no Ludendorff had ever seen. Then the inconceivable happened. The masses were standing from 9 in the morning in the cold and fog. Somewhere their leaders were sitting and conferring. The fog lifted and the masses were still standing. Their leaders conferred. Noon came and in addition to the cold, hunger came. And the leaders

conferred. The masses were feverish with excitement: they wanted one deed, even one word to calm their excitement. But nobody knew what to say. Because the leaders were conferring. The fog came again and with it the dusk. The masses went home sad. They wanted great things, but they had done nothing.[13]

Had the hastily formed "revolutionary committee," made up of leading members of the USPD, KPD and the Revolutionary Shop Stewards, taken action on Monday (January 6) or at latest Tuesday (January 7) the government could have been deposed. At that moment the overwhelming majority of Berlin workers appear to have welcomed this idea. Of course, a government based on the left-wing USPD, the KPD and revolutionary shop stewards in Berlin would have been limited to the national capital and maybe a few industrial centers.[14] Would this have led to a "Berlin Commune" that would have been smothered in blood by the military? Alternatively, could it have been the spark that began a second, socialist, revolution? We will never know with absolute certainty and cases have been made for both possibilities.

It is clear the revolutionary leaders had no plan or vision of what to do next. Even Rosa Luxemburg, called the "best brain since Marx,"[15] was initially opposed to an uprising, then unsure, decided to support a bid for power, and finally resigned to defeat.[16] Some people had occupied buildings and erected barricades, a quaint but useless tribute to past revolutions in an era of artillery.

Some saw the hand of the government in the useless occupations. Paul Frölich, later a member of the KPD Central Committee, cites the findings of a Committee of Investigation appointed by the Prussian Diet which, in his words, "established that all the newspaper occupations had been carried out under the leadership of agents in the pay of the Berlin Commandant's office, or, at any rate, by highly dubious elements. At the head of the group occupying *Vorwärts* was the waiter Alfred Roland, who was later exposed as a dangerous *agent provocateur*."[17]

The truth of this charge we may never know. It could be wishful thinking on the part of a revolutionary who is loath to admit that his comrades could get carried away in the heat of the moment or it may have an element of truth. Meanwhile, the government mobilized 10,000 supporters on the streets around the *Reichskanzlerpalais* to protect the government from the revolutionary forces. This was sufficient as the great majority of the government's opponents wanted to avoid a bloodbath.

Moreover, this points to an alternative strategy for the SPD government that could have avoided use of the *Freikorps*. Since German Social Democracy still had many supporters, particularly outside Berlin, the party could have called out their own members throughout Germany as a sign of their popular support. If large enough, such demonstrations would have had the potential to push the far left off the streets in a mainly peaceful fashion. But, the SPD leaders did not trust their own members or the depth of their support among the common people.

The SPD was not unique in ignoring average people; that charge can fairly be leveled against the left as well. By January 9, there was a unity movement within factories and workplaces in Berlin and other urban areas. This movement from below proposed overcoming party lines by the "removal of the old, discredited leaders with the dual aim of avoiding fratricidal fighting and implementing socialist policies."[18]

In mass meetings, delegations were elected, largely with equal numbers of SPD, USPD and KPD delegates, to demand the resignation of the government and the leaders of all political parties in order to end the fighting. In addition, they wanted management of work to be taken over by workers committees, the unification of all three socialist parties, and new elections to the workers' councils.

Even most SPD members supported this movement as evidenced by the adoption of two resolutions in the plenary session of the Greater Berlin municipal workers' council delegates, on January 10, which demanded the resignation of the government and the cooperation of all workers regardless of party affiliation.[19] Only the USPD supported this grassroots initiative while both the KPD and the revolutionary shop stewards stood in opposition. Of course, the opposition of the SPD leadership was never in question. Not for the first time, it appears the average people were more insightful than their better-known leaders.

For their part, the Social Democratic leadership did not want to negotiate or compromise. They wanted to use force to restore order.[20] If in spite of its violent rhetoric, the revolutionary left was normally hesitant to spill blood, the government had no such scruples. Gustav Noske, who had helped manage the situation in Kiel in early November, was willing to use the tools on hand to suppress the opposition. And, the tools he had on hand were the troops of the viciously right-wing *Freikorps*. This ensured a reign of terror but unlike the French Revolution, an example so often cited by all sides, it would come from the far right.

Various *Freikorps* units serving under the general direction of Gustav Noske seized upon the previous week's fighting as an excuse to decapitate the revolution.[21] Around 9 p.m. on January 15, Rosa Luxemburg, Karl Liebknecht and Wilhelm Pieck, were arrested by Freikorps troops in the Berlin suburb of Wilmersdorf. They took the three KPD leaders to the Eden Hotel for questioning. That same evening, Luxemburg and Liebknecht were murdered while Pieck escaped.[22] Luxemburg's body was thrown into a canal and not found for months. The poet Bertolt Brecht certainly spoke for many people when he wrote:

EPITAPH, 1919

Red Rosa now has vanished too.
Where she lies is hid from view.
She told the poor what life is about
And so the rich have rubbed her out.[23]

Major Waldemar Pabst, who supervised the assassinations of Luxemburg and Liebknecht, wrote in his memoirs that on January

17 he reported directly to the government. Pabst even claimed to have personally been congratulated by Ebert and Noske and shaken their hands.[24] Historians can't verify his claims but it is clear that the Social Democratic leadership was glad to be rid of both revolutionaries. At a SPD rally in Kassel, Scheidemann almost openly welcomed the murders in a speech given on January 16, 1919 by saying they "have fallen victim to their own bloody terror tactics."[25] Further, he compared Liebknecht to a "mad brother" threatening an innocent family who therefore had to be shot.[26]

Most likely encouraged by these unpunished acts of brutality, other assassinations quickly followed. Luxemburg's comrade and sometimes lover, Leo Jogiches, labored to bring the guilty to justice. Although his efforts were marked with a great deal of success in uncovering evidence, Jogiches was himself murdered in March.[27] A monarchist murdered Kurt Eisner, head of the Bavarian revolutionary government, on February 21.[28] Eugen Leviné was at least given a trial before being shot after the fall of the Bavarian Soviet Republic.[29]

Hugo Haase, long time socialist and leading USPD member, was shot on his way to parliament in October 1919.[30] Early 1919 also saw Heinrich Dorrenback, a former leader of the People's Naval Division who had been arrested, "shot while attempting to escape."[31] This happened a lot to leftist prisoners captured by government forces. Unless one holds to the rather unlikely idea that few officers knew how to secure their captives, it was an expression frequently employed to excuse political murder.

Naturally, all of these victims were vilified in the most false and vicious terms by the racist and anti-Semitic *Freikorps*, their enablers in the press, pay masters in big business and supporters in the government administration. What was true of the famous was, if anything, even truer for ordinary and anonymous people who fell to the counter-revolutionary violence. Although not singled out by name, these seldom-discussed fatalities have often been dismissed collectively.

Robert Leinert, a leading member of the SPD, was quick to believe the worst about the revolutionary crowds in Berlin during the January Days. Leinert argued, the revolutionary left was "no longer ideological, it has ... attracted a considerable number of criminals."[32] One American writer employed numerous pejoratives to describe the German revolutionaries. He labelled them "without much fear of contradiction" as "the 'crazy fringe,' 'army deserters and stragglers;' the 'utopian radicals;' the 'dregs of the German labor movement'—in short, the 'proletariat of rogues.'"[33] Another rightist author was more concise when he attacked the Berlin crowds as "the scum of the great capital."[34]

Let us examine what we know about the social background of those who were present during street fighting in Berlin. Could the crowds have been heavily made up of criminals or riffraff? If the available evidence is to be believed, the answer is no. One study gives great insight into the social structure of those who fell during mass actions from November 1918 to January 1919.[35] The data from this study conclusively proves that most of those killed in the January fighting were skilled or semi-skilled workers. Within this demographic, the most frequent occupations were: locksmith, turner, or toolmaker—all three being skilled trades within the metal industry.[36] Nor were these occupations the result of war-related temporary dislocation, since the fathers of the fallen had been primarily employed in similar labor activities.[37]

A second display of radical defiance took place in Bremen where members of the city's workers' council declared a Councils' Republic in late January. This new Bremen government was led by three USPD members, three Communists and three unaffiliated soldiers. Laws were passed to help the unemployed and raise wages. At the end of January official government soldiers attacked Bremen and the "Bremen Soviet Republic" was defeated on February 4, 1919. Just like in the capital, in less than a month the new Social Democratic led government in Berlin allowed their troops to use excessive violence to prove their control of power.[38]

The city of Hamburg also suffered deadly violence in early 1919, though not nearly to the extremes seen in Berlin and Bremen. During Easter 1919, there were militant protests in working-class neighborhoods and attempts to free prisoners held in police custody. The Hamburg police felt they were under attack and called upon some 600 military reinforcements. In contrast to the attitude shown by other organs of government repression, the police protested that "our task is to fight criminals and protect property ... We want to serve everyone."[39] These may have been only self-serving words but the *Freikorps* seldom pretended to be anything but butchers. It is interesting, and may well speak to the pressure of popular opinion, that the Hamburg police felt the need to justify their actions. Although there were 18 deaths, the reign of terror that swept Berlin and later Munich were both bloodier.

Since November 1918, the local Workers' Council in which the USPD had played a major part dominated Halle. Eyewitness Oskar Hippe reported that in March 1919 the government transferred a *Freikorps* unit under the pretense that calm Halle needed to have peace restored. The Trade Unions, USPD and KPD resented this imposition and demanded the troops be withdrawn. In response, the Freikorps rounded up all visible resisters whether trade unionists, USPD or KPD members. Large numbers of workers reacted by going out on strike. Of course, the strike leadership was then arrested. After three days of clashes that took place throughout Halle, the resistance was broken and hundreds dragged off to prison.[40]

If Berlin had been a tragedy, Munich was first a farce followed by tragedy. Kurt Eisner's USPD had been defeated in the January 1919 election and he was going to announce his resignation when he was shot dead by a right-wing aristocrat. This act of senseless violence caused unrest and, combined with news of a left-wing revolution in nearby Hungary, encouraged far-leftists, including anarchists, to seize control. After the SPD failed in its attempt to form a new government, on April 6, 1919 USPD members and anarchists proclaimed a Bavarian Soviet Republic.

As Ernst Toller, a playwright and the one-time leader of this ill-fated venture, later realized, this "Soviet Republic was a foolhardy *coup de main* on the part of the bewildered workers, an attempt to salvage the lost German Revolution."[41] Like Eisner's government before, this new collection of assorted radicals was unable to provide even the most basic government services. This Soviet Republic was inundated with even more cranks than usually appeared in such times of crisis. As Toller admitted, some "believed that the root of all evil was cooked food, others the gold standard, others unhygienic underwear, or machinery, or the lack of a compulsory universal language, or multiple stores, or birth control."[42]

Nor were many of the officials of the new government more firmly grounded in reality. Responsibility for Foreign Affairs was given to Dr Franz Lipp, a man who had repeatedly been in and out of psychiatric hospitals. In his new capacity, Lipp declared war on Switzerland over the Swiss refusal to lend 60 locomotives to the Republic and cabled V. I. Lenin that the Social Democrats had run off with the key to his office bathroom.[43] Though he claimed to be a good friend of the Pope, his colleagues had him quietly bundled off to a sanatorium.[44]

This farce had a run of fewer days than some of Toller's more unsuccessful plays. On Sunday, April 12, 1919, the KPD took power led by Eugen Leviné. The Communists had opposed the creation of the Bavarian Soviet Republic and accurately prophesied that it must collapse in rivers of blood.[45] The KPD leadership in Berlin warned against taking power in Munich. But, Leviné and his followers went against the advice of cooler heads despite their own earlier warnings about such a move.[46] It gave the Social Democratic government the excuse they had looked for to shatter the rebels in Bavaria. In fact on April 27, even before the government troops reached the outskirts of the city, the Soviet government was proclaimed to be over.[47]

Although supporters of Leviné did shoot some far right-wing hostages, the overwhelming violence was on the part of the government troops and the *Freikorps*. Of the over 1,000 estimated dead from the period of repression, only 58 of that number were government troops.[48] The majority of the fatalities did not result from combat but were the result of prisoners and even innocent bystanders being executed by the invading troops. One Officer boasted of whipping a working-class woman until there was no white spot left on her back. Further, there are accounts of *Freikorps* troops "shooting communist women 'for target practice.'"[49] It was, as one historian has commented, "a frenzy of fatal violence."[50]

Although armed force and physical violence is the final weapon of any state, no government can last long on terror alone. As Talleyrand, a French politician, once said, it "is possible to do many things with a bayonet, but one cannot sit on one."[51] In other words, governments need to be perceived as legitimate; they need a narrative to explain why they should be in power. For the SPD, the legitimizing goal was to achieve socialism for Germany. Not wild, chaotic socialism that leads to tyranny like Russia but orderly and well organized socialism.

Thus, the commanding heights of the economy were to be "socialized." But not right away. On December 18, 1918, Rudolf Hilferding, a renowned Marxist economist in his day, argued, "I am convinced that the idea of simple confiscation would be incorrect ... we cannot immediately organize the whole of production in a socialist way."[52] When there was a general strike in Berlin in March 1919, the government sought to undercut it and declared: "Socialization is Here!" The proclamation of March 4, 1919 promised universality in government explaining, "in other words all of us, will control this German communal economy. The Reich will take care that the economy is run everywhere in the common interest, and nowhere in the private interests of the capitalists. And that is socialism."[53]

At this same time, delegates attending the first national USPD saw that the government had plastered posters on the walls of Berlin, claiming "Socialization is on the march." "It always remained on the march," as Toni Sender wryly noted, "and never arrived at the goal."[54] In fact, the plan was to socialize precisely nothing. The government allowed big business to bog down the process with countless petty details.[55] Karl Kautsky complained in an April 1919 speech that there was "called into existence a Socialisation Commission but merely as an advisory body and it narrowed its sphere of competence so far as to make it insignificant."[56] He could have added that many of the appointed members were hostile to an act of socialization from the outset.

The SPD continued to propagate a myth: that as soon as the details could be worked out, the large capitalists would be expropriated. When the Weimar Constitution was approved in August 1919, it included Article 156 stating that laws could be passed to take over capitalist enterprises. All the talk of socialism being thrown around by German Social Democracy made many think it was just a matter of patience. Actually, as one scholar commented, the "only active policy of economic transition which was attempted was the socialization of industries. But this attempt, on the whole, remained in the sphere of theory, and the *Sozialisierungsgetz* of 1919 meant practically the pigeonholing of socialization."[57]

The bloody repression of 1919 would cost German Social Democracy support while allowing the tiny KPD to become a mass party. Herbert Marcuse, a noted philosopher later in American exile, was a member of a soldiers' council as a young man in Germany. In addition, Marcuse was a member of the SPD from 1917 till 1919. He resigned in protest after the suppression of the Berlin left in January 1919, and said, 50 years later, "from then on I have criticized this party's politics."[58] Heinz Brandt, a post-World War II radical arrested in East Germany who later became a West German trade union official, likewise testifies that the January repression was an important factor in his political development.[59]

The bitterness, despair and hopelessness that the repression of 1919 caused many to feel was captured in fictional form by Nobel Prize winner Heinrich Böll. In his *Group Portrait with Lady*, one character recounts that he carried a photo of Rosa Luxemburg in his wallet like a saint's picture. This imaginary worker tells how, "in 1914 German history came to an end for me and then of course they killed Rosa Luxemburg, had her killed, those gentlemen of the Social Democratic Party."[60]

If the common people often got empty promises, the old functionaries got to continue to run much of Germany. Even the Foreign Service, unequivocally unsympathetic to the revolution and later the republic, carried on unchanged despite being made up of "a rather enclosed elite of conservatively disposed, largely aristocratic diplomats."[61] Not only were the old diplomats, police, officer corps, judges, industrialists, large land owners, accountants, bureaucrats and bankers able to endure, they looked to the government to help them prosper.

In a letter to SPD leader Friedrich Ebert, General Groener pointed out that the new regime might prove to be a blessing for the ideals of the old military leadership. The opportunity opened up by the revolution, "must be exploited under all circumstances in order to make the German dream of a powerful state, encompassing the whole German race, and based on a strong central power, reality."[62] Despite having different ultimate goals, the new government and the military agreed on many things like the centralization of war ministries in 1919. This is part of a narrative that provides "an alternative to the views of conflictual relations between the officer corps and the Republic, and especially between the officer corps and the SPD."[63]

This all may help explain why so many rejected German Social Democracy. It does not explain why so many continued to be SPD members, supporters and voters. First, it is important to remember that the Social Democratic Party was more than a political party; it was at the same time a culture, a way of life. At any given time, many or even most SPD rank and file members might accept criticism of their leaders. They typically thought the problem was this or that bad leader not their party, and certainly not their alternative socialist culture.

One author long ago identified this apparently contradictory position. During the height of World War II's fury, Evelyn

Anderson wrote that ordinary workers saw leaders like Noske as a type of foul growth that should be cut out of the Social Democratic body. The party itself was, however, something completely different:

> The Party—that was he himself and his colleague who worked on the same bench, his friend from the same tenement house who thought and felt like himself, who had built up this Party in the past and fought in its ranks and watched it growing stronger and stronger until, at last, it was the head of the nation. To this Party, as they saw and knew it, most German workers, in particularly Trade Unionists, remained loyal.[64]

Objectively, the revolution led to a remarkable upsurge in trade union membership. This reassured average trade unionists while further tying any number of trade union leaders to the new system. Even the most radical critic of Social Democracy's post-war behavior tended to see the three fold, almost four fold, surge in union membership as a real sign of progress.

Table 6.2 Membership in trade unions

Year	Free trade unions	Christian trade unions	Hirsch-dunckersche trade unions[a]	Total
1913	2,574,000	343,000	107,000	3,024,000
1914	2,076,000	283,000	78,000	2,437,000
1915	1,159,000	176,000	61,000	1,396,000
1916	967,000	174,000	58,000	1,199,000
1917	1,107,000	244,000	79,000	1,430,000
1918	1,665,000	405,000	114,000	2,184,000
1919	5,479,000	858,000	190,000	6,527,000
1920	7,890,000	1,077,000	226,000	9,193,000

Note: [a] These were liberal trade unions who sought to avoid conflict and radical political involvement.

Source: Jürgen Kuczynski, *Die Geschichte der Lage der Arbeiter Unter Dem Kapitalismus*, vol. IV, Berlin: Akademie Verlag, 1967: 243.

Moreover, the very real gains of the revolution, at least partially, satisfied many while they patiently waited for the parliamentary road to wind its way to socialism. Many did not see that the "march to socialization" was leading nowhere. Ordinary women and men thought that what was happening was an orderly, if uneven, transformation to the new world they had so long been promised. This was more than mere wishful thinking.

In 1919, a pattern emerged of misery and frustration leading to angry actions. This cycle was sometimes provoked by the authorities as pretense to repress the masses. Since "socialists" led the government many people remained confused. Could the traditional party of Labor be ordering people shot? Were the victims of state violence criminals as it was often alleged? When a person asked her friends, co-workers or comrades such questions, the answers varied. What is clear a century later was at the time confusing and wrapped in a fog of rumor and speculation.

Yet there were real and dramatic changes. The monarchy had been abolished. The republic that had been a dream since 1848 was now a reality. This would be a republic that gave all citizens, women as well as men, the right to vote. Remember, the Weimar Republic had the most liberal, democratic constitution in the world. Real power, apparently, was held in the hands of elected representatives; a far cry from the days when the Reichstag was a fig leaf for absolutism. The old militarists had seemingly, if not actually, been pushed from power. The great lords of Industry and Land must surely be replaced? Many confused the SPD in office with the common people being in power.

7

Women in the War and the Revolution

Women have been hidden from history. So it is no surprise that the German Revolution is typically given a male-centric narrative. Despite it seldom being discussed, "gender was a critical dimension of the transformations of 1918/19."[1] It is not unexpected to find female agency absent from so many narratives, but this absence produces an inaccurate and incomplete account history. Among others, Clara Zetkin made a powerful case for the centrality of women to the German revolution. Less than two weeks after the overthrow of Imperial Germany, on November 22, 1918, Zetkin published her article "The Revolution—Thanks to the Women" in *Rote Fahne*.

This emphasis on female workers was echoed by Rosa Luxemburg in a letter to Zetkin on November 24. The letter proposes a daily supplement to *Rote Fahne* directly focused on female readers, or maybe a separate women's paper. Luxemburg emphasizes the importance of agitation among women insisting that "it is such an urgent matter! Every day lost is a sin."[2] Five days later, she writes again begging for Zetkin to write a "general leaflet about women workers and revolution."[3] What Zetkin and Luxemburg understood was that without women, radical potentialities would be greatly reduced.

If some on the left praised women as revolutionaries, the right heaped scorn on them as traitors who were behind "the stab in the back." One emerging pillar upholding this myth was the claim that women and children were responsible for the military failure on Christmas Eve to overwhelm the People's Naval Division.[4] The right blamed radical women for Germany's defeat in the war. In nationalist circles, female workers on the home front were singled out as undermining the war effort. One rightist woman, Paula Mueller-Otfried, criticized working-class women's "grumbling letters and moaning and groaning" for undermining soldiers' morale.[5] The central role women played in the revolution was acknowledged by both military and *Freikorps* leaders, though in this case such acknowledgment was leveled as a perverse insult. The officers denounced revolutionary crowds as "feminine" and complained that the presence of women made their troops reluctant to open fire.[6] The upheavals of war and revolution may have roused deep fears among male nationalists of a loss of masculinity and perhaps an "unconscious hatred of women."[7]

This latent hatred manifested itself during the 1919 counter-revolutionary violence where women appeared to be targeted for special abuse. The right's fear of female "subversion" of soldiers was more than unfounded paranoia. During June 1916, street protests in Nuremburg, male auxiliary policemen mainly defied orders and joined the largely female crowds. Toward the end of the war, soldiers made sure to absence themselves in advance of demonstrations or simply took the side of the women.[8] What conservative nationalists saw as disloyalty was considered a noble defense of the working class by radical socialists.

The struggle for women to attain their own agency was part of a long historical process. Industrialization had resulted in increasing numbers of female workers, particularly important were women factory workers. This in turn began to impact the German working class in ways both positive and negative. With women entering industry in the later part of the nineteenth century, middle- and upper-class reformers began to rant about all the ills they associated with female factory labor. As early as the turn of the twentieth century, the German government had banned female work between 8:30 p.m. and 5:30 a.m. Women were only allowed to work a maximum of eleven hours during the week or ten on Saturdays.[9]

Hardworking women were often recast as delinquent or spendthrift mothers and wives neglecting their families. There were calls for "protection" of women by reformers. This in effect, in the words of feminist Alice Saloman, "persecuted women struggling for economic independence and social equality."[10] Put differently, protecting women from working outside the house actually meant returning them to a submissive role within the family household.

Not that is how those of better income, status and education tended to view matters. Their general attitude towards German working women can be seen by looking at their public writings. In 1911, for example, middle-class readers were told that even when women "devote themselves completely to working for a living, the main occupation for most women, by contrast to men, is and remains marriage and the family."[11] Tellingly, later historians have characteristically relied on these accounts, written by those criticizing working women a century ago, to draw their conclusions about the status of laboring women of that time period. Unfortunately, this type of historical inquiry is dependent upon an artificial middle-class rubric that already judged women workers as wanting.

The private family sphere was set against the idea of women in public employment by middle-class females. The latter spent a good deal of effort creating an imagined community of German *Hausfrauen* (housewife). Authors of so-called women's magazines and books on care of the home attempted to establish a set of standards that could be applied to all German women regardless of region or social group.[12] Naturally, poor or working-class women were important targets of "bourgeois reformers, who were anxious to teach them 'proper' methods of housekeeping."[13] Another bourgeois feminist "exalted motherhood as the fundamental, life-sustaining social labor" for all German women.[14] It would not be unkind to say that these women did not understand working-class females nor did bourgeois women try to comprehend the life of their social "inferiors."

It would be a mistake to think of working women as mere passive victims waiting for reforms enacted by upper-class men or women, great or small. Female workers developed a culture apart from those of bourgeois feminists and other middle-class reformers. For example, they accepted out-of-wedlock births and typically refused to accept the shame such occurrences had for better off Germans. By the time of World War I, on average 9 to 10 percent of all births were illegitimate, with this rate being much higher in industrial areas.[15]

In many arenas, women, especially working-class females, were becoming more aware of controlling their own bodies and sexuality.[16] Their extensive use of birth control, while certainly influenced by economic conditions, was at the same time an expression of control over their bodies. One study conducted from 1911–13 found 64 percent of working-class women using birth control, including abortion.[17] Other studies came up with like numbers; so, it would seem that "65 to 75 percent of the working class practiced some kind of birth control."[18]

To put this in a comparative context, in 2010 the US Department of Health and Human Services found 62 percent of American women using contraception.[19] This, despite the wide availability of the pill and other birth control methods, makes one wonder if the claims of a "sexual revolution" are overblown. The prevalence of sexual and reproductive agency already shown by working-class women of Germany by the early twentieth century emphasizes their independence.

Abortion was strictly illegal in Imperial Germany. Still, as industrialization produced urbanization and proletarianization, women turned more frequently to abortion. In the period 1882–94, it is estimated there were 14.14 abortions per 100,000 live births. By 1897–1914, this had more than doubled to 38.79 pregnancy terminations for every 100,000 births. In large cities, the increase was even more dramatic with Hamburg seeing a rise of abortions from 28.10 to 53.75 and Berlin going from 59.59 to 220.95.[20] Naturally, religion and cultural traditions meant there were marked differences in women's response to undesired pregnancy. Catholic women were more likely to abandon unwanted children while Protestants were more likely to have abortions. German women of Jewish origin were less likely than average to do either.[21] There was a rapid growth in female prostitution in the late nineteenth and early twentieth century. Typically a sex worker would be a woman in her early or mid-twenties, who turned to prostitution after failing to find work in other fields. Unlike the hypocritical public horror expressed by the upper levels of German society, the working class was more understanding that sex work was a means to feed oneself or one's family.[22] As August Bebel commented, the number of prostitutes "increases at the same rate which the number of working women increases, who find employment in various lines of trade at starvation wages."[23] In other words, there is a direct connection between low wages, lack of employment for women and the rise of prostitution.[24] To many on the left, prostitutes were workers just like any others, not fallen women, and this led to later attempts to organize these women into trade unions to defend their rights.[25]

At the same time, German proletarian women defended their own definition of sexuality in both individual and collective protests against rape or sexual harassment by factory supervisors. This took different forms: reporting incidents to the union or factory inspectors, spreading the word among other women so they would be on guard, and even strike actions. In 1902 in Düsseldorf, a furious crowd, made up of both women and men, demonstrated at the home of a master weaver who had sexually assaulted a female subordinate. One worker died and four were sent to jail as a result of their actions. Another example is from 1905, where female workers along with male comrades went on strike in a Bocholt mill to demand the firing of an overseer who raped several women.[26]

Despite these and other occasions in which male workers supported their female counterparts, there remained a large degree of anti-feminism within the male proletariat of Germany. These men believed that having women in the workforce drove wages down and caused stress within the working-class family.[27] This attitude was sharply opposed to the theory put forth by Marxists who believed that an increase in women's work would lead to their, and ultimately everyone's, emancipation. August Bebel, one of the founders of German Social Democracy, dealt a blow against antifeminism with the publication of his *Woman under Socialism* in 1879.[28] The German language editions of this popular book had been reprinted over 50 times by Bebel's death in 1913. In addition to such high sales, Bebel's work was for many years the title "most borrowed from workers' libraries in Germany, and it continued to serve as a major socialist primer into the first decades of the twentieth century."[29] For many working women, the title "encouraged identification with socialism as the mean to women's emancipation."[30]

As Fredrick Engels later wrote in his widely read *Origin of the Family, Private Property and the State*:

> The emancipation of woman will only be possible when woman can take part in production on a large, social scale, and domestic work no longer claims anything but an insignificant amount of her time. And only now has that become possible through modern large-scale industry, which does not merely permit of the employment of female labor over a wide range, but positively demands it, while it also tends towards ending private domestic labor by changing it more and more into a public industry.[31]

Nor were Engels and Bebel the only German socialists who promoted this view. There were pivotal women like Clara Zetkin, Toni Sender and Luise Zietz.

Engels's standing in the movement, and the popularity of his, and Bebel's, arguments meant that women's emancipation became an official part of the SPD program from 1890 onward. As always, matters were not so simple as passing a resolution or writing a plank in a party platform. All the same, objective conditions conspired with the pro-working woman stance of the party to attract an increasing number of female members.

Table 7.1   Survey of female SPD membership, 1906–19

Year	Female SPD members	Percentage women in SPD
1906	6,460	1.7
1907	10,943	2.1
1908	29,458	5.6
1909	62,259	9.8
1910	82,642	11.5
1911	107,693	12.9
1912	130,371	13.4
1913	141,115	14.4
1914	174,751	16.1
1915	?	?
1916	107,336	24.8
1917	66,608	27.4
1918	70,659	28.3
1919	206,354	20.4

Source: Werner Thönnessen, *The Emancipation of Women: The Rise and Decline of the Women's Movement in German Social Democracy, 1863–1933*, London: Pluto Press, 1973: 116.

Notice that the highest percentage, but not absolute number, of female SPD members was in 1918, the year of the German Revolution. If we can take this as indicative of female political involvement, and maybe radicalization, this suggests that women played a critical role during the overthrow of the old regime.

It has been argued that gender equality could not be truly "instituted in the SPD, influenced and bound up as this mass party was with the institutions and ideology of the patriarchal order in which it was imbedded."[32] In day-to-day life, antifeminism persisted in large sections of male workers. Toni Pfülf, a socialist female activist, saw the situation as contradictory. She explains that lip service was paid to women's equality ideologically but "in their heart of hearts, the great majority of the organized [male] work force does not favour liberation ... Sexual pride wins out over principles."[33]

Forgetting the importance of women to historical development is more of a rule than an exception. The German Revolution is not one of the exceptions. This is easy to explain, not only because of the weight of past traditions, but because World War I played a key role in revolution in Germany. And, war is typically told as an almost exclusively male experience. Of course, even if there were some truth to this narrative as concerns the shell cratered trenches, women in wartime dominated the home front, an arena of drastic social change. Labor shortages allowed female workers to break into previously male-only occupations, from bus driving to metal working.

Home life during the war was its own type of warfront—less visible but just as important for the German war effort. It was a front where death came from disease and hunger not bullets and artillery shells. Female workers were on the frontlines working in a myriad of jobs and holding society together as wives, mothers and daughters. Women were among the first to break with the wartime social truce and take to the streets to protest.

In the first few months of the war, August and September 1914, the Berlin police put a major focus on food lines, largely populated by working-class women. Soon shortages caused public disturbances that the police had difficulty controlling without resorting to outright violence. One Berlin cop commented that the government didn't concern itself enough with the situation of the workers. "It is no wonder," the policeman concluded, that crowds mainly of women, "are storming shops and taking what they can."[34]

In March 1915, the International Socialist Women's conference was held in Berne, Switzerland. Clara Zetkin's fierce anti-war resolution was passed. In this resolution she blamed the war on the capitalists and urged socialist women of all countries to unite for peace.[35] Zetkin forcefully argued that the fight against the war had to be intertwined with the struggle for socialism.[36] Given the strength of wartime censorship, how would anyone in Germany read Zetkin's words? After a few copies were smuggled across the border, and sympathetic printers were found to reproduce the resolution, there remained the question of illegal distribution. All this time, the military authorities were looking for any publication containing the Berne conference women's appeal. Radical women had to operate covertly if they wanted to get the word out.

In Frankfurt, distribution of the anti-war appeal was headed by a working-class woman named Elizabeth. At a clandestine meeting of women, she assigned different districts to the various female antiwar activists. She instructed everyone to wear long capes to conceal the flyers. Urging caution, she then said, "work is to be started each day after sunset. Inconspicuously, we must see to it that the leaflets find their way into the homes."[37] None of them were caught in the act although the police later arrested two female comrades suspected of being peace advocates. Without evidence of guilt, they were soon released.

Until late 1916, the SPD's women's paper titled *Die Gleicheit* (The Equality) pushed against war as far as possible under conditions of military censorship. Under the editorship of Clara Zetkin and other antiwar women, *Die Gleicheit* was a troublesome thorn in the side of the conservative Social Democratic leaders. Clara Zetkin was forced to resign the editorship and a less political paper appeared until it folded in 1922. Nonetheless, *Die Gleicheit*, under Zetkin's direction had helped consolidate a militant female wing within German Social Democracy.

Another key female radical and contributor to *Die Gleichheit* was Luise Zietz. She had been the first woman selected to be on the SPD party executive and, with Hugo Haase, was one of the only two radicals.[38] It was Zietz who successfully proposed, with a second by Zetkin, the establishment of International Women's Day at a meeting of the Second International in Copenhagen in 1910. Zietz was later one of the most outspoken opponents of pro-war Social Democrats. She was active in promoting the idea that antiwar socialists should break with the SPD leaders. Finally, with the creation of the group that would become the USPD in 1917, radical Luise Zietz was expelled from the SPD executive.[39]

It was not just Zietz; German Social Democracy lost many of its most gifted women because of the party schism.[40]

Table 7.2   Circulation of *Die Gleichheit*, 1913–20

Year	Circulation
1913	112,000
1914	124,000
1915	46,500
1916	35,500
1917	19,000
1918	28,000
1919	33,000
1920	11,000

Source: Werner Thönnessen, *The Emancipation of Women: The Rise and Decline of the Women's Movement in German Social Democracy, 1863–1933*, London: Pluto Press, 1973: 119.

But, it was not only highly placed women who fought for peace and social change. During the war, ordinary women often acted openly in defiance of the government. The authorities were hesitant to arrest women for fear of compromising already shaky morale yet the number of female convictions for protests skyrocketed. In the year before World War I, female convictions for disturbing the peace, participation in riots and like offenses was only 187. By 1917, the number of women convicted for the same crimes rose to 1,028.[41] Police informers warned of the key role women played in radical groups like the USPD and the *Spartaksubund*. As time went on, the police became increasingly concerned about revolutionary ideas being shared in purportedly non-political Social Democratic "women's reading evenings."[42]

One can glimpse the frantic activity of those revolutionary women, not yet detained by the authorities, in a letter dated January 14, 1916 from Käte Duncker to her husband, Hermann. She explains she is working hard to organize revolutionary resistance to the war. The next day, Käte Duncker tells Hermann she will speak about the prospects of the Women's movement after the war.

> On Tuesday, [January 18, 1916], I speak in the afternoon about war socialism. On the 19th [she will discuss] with the youth of Neukölln [a neighborhood in Berlin] about the international youth movement. On the 20th, [she will participate in a] discussion evening with the youth in the north. At the 23rd Workers' Educational School, on the 24th reading evening in Neukölln. On the 25th Steglitz ... On the 26th continuation in Neukölln of discussion of the 19th, on the 27th ... On the 28th, reading evening in the Steglitz youth hostel. On the 30th Worker Educational School—You see, I'm not lazy.[43]

Käte Duncker was only one of numerous devoted female radicals. In Frankfurt in 1916, as Toni Sender reported, for example, "the bulk of the opposition to the war was formed by women."[44]

The global armed conflict sucked men out of German industry leaving vacancies filled by women. Even before 1914, trade unions had become increasingly packed with women. One female organizer even joked that the day might come where men would have to fight for equal rights in the union. While it didn't come to that, women were the bulk of wartime strikers. In 1916, 62 percent of all work stoppage participants were female and the following year saw women make up 75 percent of strikers.[45]

Even women who had what passed as good paying jobs and access to special ration supplements, like munitions workers, were protesting by early 1917. In April of that year, 200,000 workers in the war industries of greater Berlin stayed home or walked off their shift. This took courage in the middle of a war, as the Army was known to draft strikers. What is little commented on is that maybe half the strikers were women. General Groener, then the head of the armaments section of the General Staff, made a comment no doubt representative of Germany's rulers: "Our worst enemies are in our midst ... the agitators for strikes ... Whoever goes on strike when our armies are facing the enemy is a cur."[46] To the Imperial German Army, the striking women, it would appear, were no better than dogs.

It was women workers in munition factories, who were the "leading forces of the mass strikes" no later than April 1917.[47] Working-class women who were not war industry workers also played an important role. In the days before the strike, these proletarian females were on the streets protesting and, in Berlin at least, appeared to make up the majority of the demonstrating crowds.[48] When the revolution broke out in November 1918, women continued to play a critical role in radical agitation.

When the revolution made its way from the naval mutiny to the inner city districts of Berlin in November 1918, it was a combination of the underground activity of women and men. Käthe Kollwitz caught the joy, confusion and amazement most must have felt in her diary of November 9, 1918, when she wrote:

> Today it is actually happening in Berlin. This afternoon ... I walked from the zoo to the Brandenburg Gate where leaflets were being distributed announcing the Kaiser's abdication. A demonstration moved through the gate and I joined ... We moved to unter den Linden. Trucks passed full of soldiers and sailors. Red flags. I saw soldiers who ripped off their cockades [decorations] and laughing tossed them to the ground. So this is really happening. We experience it but can scarcely grasp it.[49]

Kollwitz thinks of her dead son Peter, "if he had lived, he would have joined them."[50]

In Hamburg, in the first days of the revolution there were scenes that seem unexpected if not unreal. Lida Gustava Heymann recounted "the convening of a large public assembly at which only women were supposed to speak." In addition to celebrating the end of the war, the monarchy, and the prospect of real social change, the women also celebrated women's right to speak in public without censorship or fear.[51] Most accounts of the German Revolution fail to note such incidents of female agency.

Likewise, the demand for women's suffrage is often presented as if it was only a concern for respectable bourgeois ladies. That may be true in the cases of the votes for women movements in England or the United States, but it was unquestionably not the case in Germany. Europe's most impressive working-class female suffrage movement took the form of female socialists in Imperial Germany.[52] This is not to say that, despite the pro-emancipation writings of Bebel, Engels, Marx and other male notables, there didn't continue to be a large number of men who were skeptical or even hostile to women's emancipation or even suffrage. As a woman named Mrs Kähler remarked at a pre-war SPD congress, "Many comrades make such a joke of the woman question that we really have to ask ourselves: Are those really Party comrades who advocate equal rights?"[53]

Male radicals even questioned if the time, effort and money spent on International Women's Day celebrations were worthwhile.[54] Liberal feminists feared police reaction if they marched and only held a single protest on the street and that was in carriages, not on foot. Socialist women, by contrast, typically ended meetings by demanding the vote and taking to the streets to press their point. In the years before the guns of war roared, these protests became more common.[55] Police sometimes responded with truncheons to break up the crowds. By the end of the bloody war and amid revolution, the Social Democrats felt the issue of equal political rights for women could no longer be delayed.

Yet, denying women the right to vote was the majority opinion of the non-socialist parties in the Reichstag to the bitter end. On November 8, 1918, the day before the Kaiser abdicated amid the turmoil of revolutionary crowds setting up councils throughout Germany, a Social Democratic proposal to extend the vote to women was actually defeated by a coalition of bourgeois parties.[56] Obviously, many have questioned how hard the SPD tried to get this passed.[57]

An insignificant delay as the Revolution gave women equal voting rights three days later. Still, it was a delay that showed once again the true face of SPD parliamentarianism. Even while the waves of revolution were sweeping away age old royal houses and defying ancient traditions, German Social Democracy continued play acting as the old order's loyal opposition. As one historian has noted that while SPD, "functionaries dithered and hesitated in the committee rooms of the Reichstag, the workers and soldiers whose demonstrations in the streets brought the revolution about, included women's suffrage in their list of demands as a matter of course."[58]

Women's struggles neither started nor ended with the war and revolution. Even something that looks like a clear victory, like gaining the right to vote, could hide a more complex reality. Marie Juchacz recalled how most female activists were unprepared for the actual fact of equal suffrage, and some even questioned its value. Juchacz was skeptical about the significance of women in the Reichstag as much of their work was "done for the waste paper basket ... [and the] economic dependence of women still exists as previously."[59]

There was more to women's struggles than getting the vote. Martha Arensee, a member of the USPD, recounted how on November 9, 1918 women surrounded work places cheering on workers who surged out before moving on to barracks to successfully call the soldiers to join the revolution.[60] While some men on the left failed to acknowledge the critical role of women in the German Revolution, males on the right usually did not forget or forgive. By the start of 1919, paramilitary groups like the proto-fascist *Freikorps* began to hold a new vision of a "feminized crowd that portrayed it as both threatening and consequently deserving of violence."[61] The beating and killing of Rosa Luxemburg on January 15, 1919 is well known but it is hardly an isolated event of violence targeted at female bodies.[62] To suppress revolutionary crowds and protests, Government troops unleashed unparalleled levels of violence against civilians including working-class women and children. To justify this, the Government had to promote an image of dangerous and brutal women who deserved no respect or mercy.[63]

This new anti-female myth was even taken up by cultural workers not associated with the *Freikorps* or the far right. For example, Max Beckmann, himself a liberal and of Jewish heritage, did a painting on the murder of Rosa Luxemburg in which he dressed her more like a prostitute in a police raid than a political revolutionary.[64] Beckmann was hardly unique in this as many male artists in postwar Germany, such as Erich Heckel and Otto Dix, portrayed women in a violent and degraded manner. Art historian, Carol Duncan has attacked "the compulsion with which women are reduced to objects of pure flesh and the lengths to which the artist goes in denying their humanity."[65] Even men among the liberal and left elite feared independent women. For the blood-thirsty men on the right, the violence went beyond paintings.

The story of the false Rosa Luxemburg gives us insight into the violence of armed counter-revolutionary men against women. After breaking up the occupation of a Berlin newspaper in January 1919, the *Freikorps* found Frau Steinbring, a mother who said she had been providing first aid. As she left the building Steinbring was greeted with punches and troops shouting: "it's red Rosa." She was hit with rifle butts, sworn at, called a Spartakus whore. Count von Westarp, one of the group's officers, remarked ominously, "this is it."[66]

Taken to a Dragoon Barracks, Steinbring and other prisoners were further abused. Six or seven female first aid workers had their clothes mostly torn off their bodies by their jailors. The soldiers continued to taunt Steinbring who they believed was Rosa Luxemburg, slapping her and hitting her with whips.[67] It seemed as if the end result would be another murder of an innocent, unarmed woman. Luckily for Frau Steinbring, a Major von Stephani intervened when a soldier raised and aimed his rifle at Steinbring. It was too public a place for such a cold blooded murder it seems.

From that point on, Major von Stephani forbid any further abuse of the prisoners and later "Rosa Luxemburg" was revealed to be the unlucky Frau Steinbring.[68] Luxemburg was not the only woman to be a target. A SPD member told Toni Sender of the USPD that army rebels were looking for her. Sender had to go into hiding to save her life.[69] In a letter to her husband on March 25, 1919, Käte Duncker commented on a newspaper report about missing radicals, which stated, "it is feared that they have also become victims of the Noske murder practice." Käte bitterly writes, "Yes, yes, it [political murder] has come a long way under the so-called democracy."[70]

Women were one of the main forces that created the revolution. Looking at the evidence, it is difficult to even imagine the German Revolution taking place in November 1918 had it not been for the mass involvement of women. Although this has habitually been neglected by history and historians, it was apparent to most people at the time. The remnants of the old order, the Freikorps, and even the nominally pro-women Social Democracy all raised alarm that ordinary women were storming onto the stage of history. From the brutal violence of the paramilitary right to the paternalism of the SPD, these forces all sought in different ways to push women off the street, out of politics, dismiss them from the factory, and push them back into the home. The typical attitude was that men should worry about politics while women tended to children and attended church. But Clara Zetkin was right: the German Revolution was only possible because of women.

8

Death Agony of the Revolution

The German Revolution didn't end neatly. Revolutions never do. Suppression of radicals by the *Freikorps* caused the streets of Berlin to run red with blood within a few months of the revolution. The repression was not limited to Berlin in January 1919. To the south in Bavaria, a rather utopian Munich Soviet Republic had been set up with a number of poets and literary figures in the government, as this collapsed in chaos the small German Communist Party took over. The government troops easily overwhelmed Munich and many of the radicals were either killed in the fighting or were arrested. Many of those arrested were executed—as was often the case with KPD leaders—while others were "shot while trying to escape." It continued to be a contested situation even after the establishment of the Weimar Republic.

In 1920, there was another lost opportunity when the right made a premature and reckless power grab. The Kapp *putsch* in March 1920 would show that the choice was not between a peaceful road to socialism led by the SPD and the wild socialism of the far left. The alternatives on offer were a complete purge of the institutions of the old order—army, courts, industrialists and so forth—or inevitably the empire would strike back. Details like forms of democracy—parliamentary versus council system—mattered far less in the immediate aftermath of the Revolution than the need to uproot the old structure of power.

In 1920, the SPD led a parliamentary government coalition elected the year before. These people may have been in office but it was less certain that they were in power. A collection of army officers, Freikorps units and right-wing nationalists decided to remove the government by force. In the early hours of March

13, 1920, Lieutenant-General Lüttwitz along with *Freikorps* units engaged in an effective *putsch* or revolt against the government in Berlin. As front man, these forces installed a far rightist, Dr Wolfgang Kapp as chancellor. General Erich von Ludendorff returned from his Swedish exile under an assumed name to take part.[1]

Their stated goals were destroying communism, which most likely meant jailing or murdering anyone with the slightest whiff of radicalism, and defying the peace agreement with the allies, the Treaty of Versailles, since it limited the size of the German military. At this point, one might be excused for thinking that Ebert's 1918 deal with the old officer corps would prove invaluable. After all, hadn't the army leaders pledged to support the government? In fact although the military leadership had no problem using violence against crowds of radical men and women, fighting against military units or the *Freikorps* was something altogether different. So, the Generals of the army high command, who had only survived the wrath of their soldiers thanks to German Social Democracy, refused to defend the republic.

It is almost enough to make you feel sorry for Gustav Noske, the SPD Minister of Defense, who seemed to be the only person in Berlin who did not see the coup approaching.[2] It was Noske who had proudly called himself a bloodhound. He had been subject to much verbal abuse, even from members of his own Social Democratic party, for ordering the massacre of the working class by the *Freikorps*. His defense was always that "this was all for the greater good of creating a new Reichswehr, a democratic Army, shorn of its traditional elitism and loyal to the Republic ... Now, the scales fell from his eyes."[3] Noske was not alone in not trusting the working class or their own SPD members but having faith in the Prussian aristocrats who led the military. Most of the SPD leadership was in either a state of denial or simply shock. Unable to think of anything else to do, Ebert and his government fled Berlin.

With the official chairs scarcely cold, the far-rightist Kapp regime set up shop in the government buildings of the capital. Much of the long-established ruling class adopted a wait and see attitude worrying over the popular reaction to the coup. General Hans von Seeckt, head of the Reichswehr, simply went home and awaited the outcome. It immediately occurred to the conspirators that they faced massive, if passive, resistance. Unlike the parliamentary bosses, Carl Legien, the conservative SPD Trade Union leader, knew what had to be done.

By noon on March 13, the first day of the Kapp putsch, Legien had initiated a call for a general strike. In language sounding more like the left-USPD or the *Spartakusbund*, the call made no whining pleas for compromise or mutual understanding. It read in part:

> Men and women! The military reaction has raised its head again ... They intend to restore absolutism, both in state and in the factories ... We are therefore calling on all workers, office employees and civil servants to go on strike immediately, All factories must be brought to a standstill ... Victory will be on the side of the working people.[4]

Even before this went out, many people were grasping any excuse to not do their jobs.

It got so bad for self-styled Chancellor Kapp that he could not find a secretary willing to type his proclamations.[5] Instead his administration had to rely on a political advisor who had a correspondence degree in dentistry but claimed to be a PhD. Another dubious character was a Hungarian who had been a preacher and Liberal MP in England before being exposed as a German spy.[6] But the proto-Nazi *putsch* had deeper problems than a few odd ball officials.

On March 14, the day after Kapp & Co. had been placed in office; it became progressively evident that the working class and other ordinary Germans were heeding the general strike call. By five o'clock that day in Berlin, there was no water, gas, trams or

electricity. In Chemnitz, the various labor parties together with
the trade unions formed a workers militia who quickly occupied
the post office, railroad station and city hall.[7] Frankfurt saw the
creation of a united revolutionary committee and the occupation
of telephone and telegraph offices. Violence by pro-*putsch* troops
resulted in death and injuries but did not break the strike.[8]

Although the KPD had initially clung to their default position
of refusing to cooperate with other workers' parties, on March 15
they had reversed themselves and threw their, admittedly limited,
weight behind the general strike. Two days into the putsch, the
Kapp–Lüttwitz administration was paralyzed. It was so bad that
the regime could not get a single poster printed. In Wilhelmshaven, sailors mutinied and arrested an Admiral along with 400
officers.[9] The *Reichsbank* rebuffed all efforts by the *putschists* to
get funds to pay for their administration since they did not have
the required signatures needed to release the cash.[10]

By Tuesday, March 16, the British government announced
they would not recognize the new rightist government.[11] The
general strike continued to choke the coup makers attempt to
govern. It was one of the first successful general strikes in history
and it squashed the right-wing conspiracy.[12] A demonstration
proving that "the people strongly united ... could accomplish
great things."[13] On March 17, 1920, Kapp hurried to a taxi with
his possessions wrapped in a sheet on top of the automobile. The
cab rushed him to the waiting plane to fly to Sweden and into the
footnotes of history.[14] So Kapp, never of great importance as an
individual, was deposed while the generals, the industrialists and
great landlords remained.

Before the misadventures of Kapp–Lüttwitz, the army and
the middle classes had regained much of their pre-war powers.
This premature rebellion divided these groups with most of the
renewed ruling class, from bankers to battalion leaders, uncertain
if not paralyzed. The Social Democratic leaders were likewise
confused and uncertain. Had not the leadership of the military
promised its support for the elected government?

A crisis had begun in the SPD when the Trade Union defied Ebert and the elected government.[15] Among large sections of the common people, most of all the working class, there was a rebellious attitude and a demand for unity. Large numbers of average SPD members demanded the removal of Noske and other right-wing Social Democrats.[16] In addition, and much more threatening than a change in personalities, rank-and-file SPD supporters were insistent on an alliance with the USPD, and some even included the KPD. The winds in Germany were blowing so fiercely from the left that even workers who identified themselves as Christians were prepared to join in a united front for democracy and against the old ruling class.

What many histories of the Kapp *putsch* miss is that the people who opposed Kapp were mainly not supporters of Ebert or Noske. They saw the general strike, demonstrations and protests as a way to finish the work begun on November 9. Lasting barely a hundred hours, the collapse of the *putsch* raised the question of what next? A majority of urban workers did not want to return to the discredited government that had allowed Kapp *putsch* to develop. The trade unions refused to call off the general strike even after the collapse of the coup until they had promises to purge the army and the old state apparatus and greatly change the system. They desired a new political system where workers would have a leading voice.

Interestingly, it was Legien and the trade unions who advocated this step. They wanted a new workers' government based on all the socialist parties and the institutions of organized labor. German Social Democracy had been so weakened by their meek response to the coup that it would have been unable to resist such a movement. For the moment, the military had fallen into chaos and would have been unlikely to be able to resist a Labor government. This workers government, while far from the council republic some hoped for, was certainly a real possibility.

It would not have been Soviet Russia but it could have purged the German army and state apparatus. At worst, this would have made the transfer of power from the old ruling class to Hitler and the Nazis less likely. At best, it would set the stage for future revolutionary developments. The failure to establish a workers' government was not so much the fault of the SPD leaders who felt impotent in the face of the trade unions. Nor were the Communists a road block as on March 21, the KPD Central Committee pledged itself to forgo armed struggle and constitute a loyal opposition.

German Social Democracy cowed by Legien and the trade unions, and the right-wing of the USPD, and even the KPD were all in favor of a workers' government. So what went wrong? The left-wing of the USPD repudiated any cooperation with the SPD, an attitude that was even attacked by the often sectarian Communists.[17] Thus, a remarkable opportunity was lost.

If the left was divided on the lesson of the *putsch*, the militaristic right was not. Unlike the hapless Kapp, General von Ludendorff did not appear to despair. He was now convinced that more ruthless leadership was needed to destroy everything the German Revolution had stood for.[18] A *Freikorps* soldier put it very bluntly when he stated that, despite the obvious errors of Kapp, "Everything would still have been all right if only we had shot more people."[19] In the 1930s, they would.

One never can say how the proposed "workers' government" would have played out. But, it is clear that the German masses were filled with confidence from their victory over the Kapp–Lüttwitz conspiracy. This was a time for action. Instead, there was a return to old parliamentary musical chairs that characterized the Weimar Republic.

Is it too harsh to say the German Revolution failed? Not from most vantage points. For the far left, it failed because they did not achieve socialism or a council republic. For more centrist leftists, it failed in not establishing a more radical democracy and curbing the excesses of Capital. Even for the right-wing Social Democrats, the revolution failed because it did not deliver the stable parliamentary system they had wanted. Most of all, for many common people, it failed because all the hopes of a new society never developed.

What was the impact of the failure of the German Revolution? For Soviet Russia, it certainly meant disaster. If it was impossible to build socialism in one country, then the defeat in Germany ultimately resulted in the failure of the revolutionary project in Russia. Yet, we do well to remember that in the short term, it did give Bolshevik Russia breathing space. As Trotsky admitted, the German Revolution, incomplete as it was, "was still strong enough to trim the claws of Ludendorff and Hoffmann. Without this operation the Soviet Republic could hardly have avoided destruction."[20]

In addition, the defeat of the German left had an impact throughout the developed capitalist world and beyond. Without a successful German model, there was only the increasingly Stalinized Russia, after 1926, for radical workers to look to for inspiration. German Social Democracy had not only alienated millions at home, they had in addition done grave damage to their brand. That is, reformist workers parties throughout the world.

The pro-war stance of many in the Socialist Parties gathered in the Socialist International had already led to tensions and splits. The German Social Democratic Party had been the largest and most powerful of all these parties and it had voted for war credits in 1914. It seems that younger members, less conditioned by decades of party loyalty and more exposed to the horrors of war, were often disproportionally represented among the dissenters who abandoned the traditional workers' parties.[21] The Bolshevik revolution in October 1917 further widened this breech as, worldwide, radicals cast their lots for, against or remained undecided about the soviet experiment.

When German Social Democracy unleashed the *Freikorps* and military units on protesting crowds and sat by while revolutionary leaders were murdered, it was another line of blood between traditional socialist labor and the newly minted communists to their left. Even in the United States, where the Socialist Party of America (SPA) had opposed the war, the events in Germany divided the movement.

Eugene V. Debs,[22] the leading socialist in the USA who had gathered nearly 1,000,000 votes for president in 1912, spoke for much of the Socialist Party of America left when he condemned the German SPD. In an article for the *Class Struggle* in February 1919, Debs said the November Revolution had meant the "day of the people" had arrived. But trying to prevent this was the SPD leadership. Debs stated:

> Then arose the cry that the people were not yet ready for their day, and Ebert and Scheidemann and their crowd of white-livered reactionaries, with the sanction and support of the fugitive Kaiser, the infamous Junkers and all the allied powers, now in beautiful alliance, proceeded to prove that the people were not yet ready to rule themselves by setting up a bourgeois government under which the working class should remain in substantially the same state of slavish subjection they were in at the beginning of the war.[23]

And this came from a person who never quit the Socialist Party to join the Communists, unlike so many others. Debs's reaction could be multiplied many fold by examples from other nations.

So why did the German Revolution fail? This is a more complex problem than can be answered by merely pointing to the treason of SPD leaders or the lack of a Bolshevik-style party. A number of factors need to be considered. First, and so obvious authors often forget to mention it, is that the new German, Social Democratic-led government ended the war, unlike the Provisional government in 1917 Russia.

The majority of the German people, as one author reminds us, who "took an active part in the Revolution had revolted first and foremost against the continuation of the War. They had revolted against those responsible for the War."[24] Unlike the Russian government that came to power in February 1917 and gambled on staying in the war, German Social Democracy understood that reality demanded the war end. The conservative Social Democrats absorbed the example of the provisional Kerensky government in Russia. They saw that above all else it had been the war continuing that allowed the Bolsheviks to come to power.

The SPD leaders were less out of touch with the common people than their counterparts in Russia. They knew that the last great offensive by the German army in March, 1918 had been a failure. General von Falkenhayn had been right when he said that Germany would ultimately lose if they failed to take Paris by Christmas 1914. Yet, as late as October 25, 1918, Ludendorff issued an order to the army urging them to hold on to the last in the name of national defense and "a peace which secures Germany her future."[25] For a time, there was a very real possibility that the old ruling class would opt for *Endkampf*.[26] That is, a final struggle. But some liberals were more fanatical than even Ludendorff. Walter Ratheanau, darling of historians because of his liberal policies in Weimar,[27] was convinced of the need for a government of national defense and mobilizing the people for a fight to the end. As late as 1919, he argued in a published essay that if only there had been a last stand, Germany would have had peace sooner and avoided the revolution.[28]

If it had not been for the revolution, the Generals and their allies might have brought down the nation around them as they did in World War II. By 1918 German troops, taking part in the last desperate roll of the dice of war on the western front, were not the great force they had once been. The underfed soldiers "fell upon the provisions they found when they took the Allies' first lines, and all the threats of their officers could not get them to move on until they were satiated."[29] It was not simply hunger, the troops had become politicized. By fall 1918, troops heading to the front were greeted by cries of "Strike breakers!" by retreating units.[30] The end of the war solved the most implacable problems facing the German common people.

Secondly, one must consider the methods used and impact of women being pushed to the sidelines. If women had been indispensable in making the revolution, the diminishing of their power would make further revolutionary advances more problematic. The new leaders and old employers played returning male soldiers off against their wives, sisters and girlfriends. Women had won the vote in part because of their important role in the 1917–18 strikes and the revolution itself. Soon, however, the talk of equal rights was replaced as the Social Democratic government eroded women's rights and began to push women out of factories and other sites of employment.[31]

Edmund Fischer, on the right-wing of the SPD, argued that the number of women workers increased only because of the war. Afterwards, married women, at very least, should leave wage-labor to men. For women, he claimed, "wage-labour cannot enrich their lives more than housework can. It is a burden and reduces the enjoyment of life."[32] Of course, Fischer's writings drew a ferocious response from Clara Zetkin. Even a relatively moderate SPD woman like Wally Zepler protested such blatant sexism. But ironically, once women had access to the ballot, many men assumed they could safely forget about the "women question."[33]

Some female workers were glad to leave factory work and return to the family household. Many were not. With the war over, there was no need to labor to produce mountains of armaments and machine guns. Despite high profits,[34] German capitalists looked forward to economic demobilization, which meant lifting of price controls, foreign trade and shedding considerable government regulation.[35] Some of the industrial bourgeoisie saw women as a reliable source of cheap labor but others saw them as being in the way. In any event, tens of thousands of women, who had worked throughout World War I, were brusquely fired. The fortunate women got two weeks' pay and a ticket back to their home town. Bluntly, they were told that they had to leave to make room for the returning men.

A good example is the Krupp works, a world famous manufacturer of death. In 1917, Krupp employed almost 30,000 women but by the end of 1918 only 300 remained. This was not always an easy task as a report pointed out, "the removal of women was not accomplished without the overcoming of considerable difficulties … it required especially vigorous measures to remove women from the coking plants …"[36] Unemployed women workers could not very well strike, could they?

By the end of the war and the revolution, women were portrayed in the press as unfaithful and adulterous creatures. Male authorities became hysterical about an imagined epidemic of venereal disease. In Hanover, for example, authorities were distressed by young women who earned high wages and worked short hours since they spent "a large part of the day and night in places of entertainment and in the streets."[37] Despite the lurid stories that spread panic and had a clearly antifeminist coloring, the rate of sexually transmitted disease appears to be the same as before the war.[38] Women were not only lied to, they were lied about.

Next, ponder that when German Social Democracy and her liberal bourgeois allies refused to purge the government apparatus of monarchists and extreme nationalists, they were signing the death warrant for their political competitors and ultimately themselves. Thus, the army, courts and so forth remained firmly in the hands of enemies of democracy and the common people. Scrutinize, for example, the judges who continued to sit and pretend to be impartial dispensers of justice. Taken as whole, there were obviously a few exceptions, these judges gave unduly harsh sentences to the left and, at most, slapped the wrist of nationalists and all assortments of rightists.

In Munich, after the suppression of the Council Republic, the courts behaved as if most of the deaths and injuries had not been caused by counter-revolutionaries. They sentenced 2200 defendants with sentences ranging from years in prison to execution. Felix Fechenbach, who had been Kurt Eisner's private secretary, was tried for high treason and given 11 years for having a role in the publication of foreign policy documents.

By contrast although responsible for an overwhelming portion of the violence, only a handful of *Freikorps* personnel were even brought to trial. The aristocrat who murdered Kurt Eisner in cold blood was lauded as a man of high ideals and the mandatory death sentence commuted to a few years. "The poster boy of Bavarian reaction," one researcher remarked, "was released in 1924, having been little more inconvenienced by his time in the Landsberg prison than was the man who moved into his vacant cell, one Adolf Hitler."[39] The behavior of the army and the Freikorps has been detailed enough to show they were no better than the judicial system.

A fourth issue to be contemplated is the fact that German Social Democracy's leaders were far more willing to employ massive violence against former leftist comrades than anyone could have imagined. Betray internationalism by supporting their nation in World War I? Of course, the SPD did. Make deals with the old establishment and ruling class for the illusion of power and minor concessions? Certainly, the leaders of German Social Democracy would have it no other way. But, murder their erstwhile comrades using the vilest nationalist thugs? That seemed unthinkable.

In hindsight, it may seem naïve but, who would think murder could be ordered or condoned by the SPD leadership. In the early stages of the revolution, even pessimistic radicals thought repression meant jail. Could they have known self-proclaimed socialists would order murder where the Kaiser had only ordered arrest? No more than the Bolshevik Party leadership could know that comrade Stalin would ultimately have them executed, except those who had died natural deaths or found safety in Norway.

In his last article before his murder on January 15, 1919, Karl Liebknecht intimates he was thinking of being thrown in the slammer, not being slaughtered. He wrote, "even if they put us in chains, we will still be here, we will remain ..."[40] The SPD-led Republic did something that the old Imperial regime could not:

deploy overwhelming military force to control the political uses of urban spaces. Along with the increased raw, brute violence, the soldiers who did the shooting and killing came to see the revolutionary crowd as "a dishonest feminized mess that was deserving of disciplining."[41] The violence was emphatically counter-revolutionary but also implicitly anti-women. This violence also created a line of blood that made future cooperation between the SPD and other workers' organization difficult. This schism caused any number of negative developments as witness the failure of the left to unite in time to fight together against the Nazis.

A fifth topic to ponder is the role of the British blockade since it continued for months after the armistice was signed. Something the western allies most certainly did not do when the Nazis established a dictatorship and tore up the Treaty of Versailles. Prolonged blockade meant protracted hunger and starvation for the German people. This fueled the nationalist passions that fed the far right while weakening the common people.

The story of Lilo Linke, an eleven-year-old girl from the poor section of eastern Berlin, gives some further depth to the problem of food shortages. Food was rationed and by the end of the war and the start of the revolution, there was never enough for the common people. This meant standing in long lines to get the meager portions allowed those with ration cards. She remembered waiting for hours in bitter cold with the winter wind howling. One winter day, Lilo Linke was standing in a huge line outside a butcher shop. Linke was malnourished and cold. Once the butcher's shop opened the crowd moved forward:

> [I thought] in half an hour I would be in the shop myself. But slowly a fear began to rise in me, right from my feet through my whole body, a fear of nothing special, just a general feeling of anxiety which seemed to empty me and hindered me from breathing. I was so lonely. I must sit down. Or try to go home. But I had to wait. I felt sick … Oh, I am dying.[42]

Fortunately for Lilo, she had just fainted. It is easy to understand if such experiences gave rise to nationalist hatreds or simply drained people to the point that they no longer had energy for the revolution.

Further, a sixth point to consider is that the food situation might have been slightly less horrific if there had not developed such a rift between the cities and the countryside. Urban revolutionaries were never able to find a suitable approach to the rural peasantry. The alliance of workers and peasants that had begun Kurt Eisner's administration in Bavaria proved to be the exception that proved the rule. The rule was that the urban radicals had little understanding of the farmers or peasants if you will.

On the last day of 1918, Rosa Luxemburg acknowledged as much in a speech to the delegates of the founding congress of the German Communist Party (KPD). The November Revolution had been only an urban revolution with the countryside relatively untouched. The peasantry, "because it has not yet been touched by the revolution, [remained] a reserve force for the counterrevolutionary bourgeoisie."[43] That said, Luxemburg had little in the way of a rural program that could have won the farm population over.

Paul Frölich was far from atypical when he denied the revolutionary potential of the German peasantry. Rather, he believed everyone in the countryside "who owns property, large or small, is outspokenly counterrevolutionary."[44] His solution was to replace the peasantry with urban workers. One of the first measures for a victorious revolution must be "the resettlement of large numbers of industrial proletarians in the countryside."[45] This is an interesting but rather wishful proposal.

A seventh consideration is that many believed the Social Democrats when they promised a fundamental transformation of the economy. Notwithstanding all limitations, abolition of the monarchy and the achievement of universal, male and female, suffrage and an extremely democratic parliamentary republic were seen as real gains. Yet, in spite of promises, "it was those at the bottom of the economic ladder ... who had to bear most painfully the social costs of German participation in the First World War."[46] By setting up a socialization commission, many thought there was going to be an orderly and peaceful road to socialism.

At an SPD party congress in June 1919, Rudolf Wissell, Minister for the Economy, criticized the complacency of the government he was a member of. He admitted that the people thought one form of domination had been replaced by another and that the new government's principles do not differ essentially from those of Imperial Germany.[47] Although slamming the views of the left, he argued for a planned economy. Wissell insisted the economy "must not receive its impulse merely from the individual's profit motive. Economic activities must be under the influence of society."[48] He was soon forced to resign his position in the cabinet.

One final factor to be contemplated is that big business changed sides depending on which way the wind was blowing. Despite being long-time ferocious enemies of trade unionism, when the working class grew rebellious the grand bourgeoisie quickly adapted. German industry recognized collective bargaining in November 1918 with the Stinnes–Legien Agreement.[49]

In autumn 1918, the great industrialists were willing to swallow any number of concessions if they thought it might save them from the revolution becoming more threatening. On November 14, 1918, Ewald Hilger spoke on behalf of the nation's steel and iron moguls, it "is not a question of money now … right now we must see that we survive the chaos."[50] For chaos, read revolution. As Victor Serge, the veteran revolutionary, recognized, the German upper class was "the most educated, the most organized, the most conscious bourgeoisie of all."[51] Thus, it may be said the German people faced a particularly cunning and dangerous enemy.

Conclusion

Standing in bread lines in 1917 Hamburg, women who had heard of the Russian Revolution said, "We only need to do what they've done in Russia, then things will be different." Such conversations could be heard on the home front, on the front lines among soldiers and sailors until the eve of the German Revolution.[1] Doing what the Russian people did is a simple idea but so hard to accomplish. From time to time, it looked as if the German Revolution might follow Russia and change the world. But, the radical potential of the German people was never developed fully.

What went wrong? Many point to the missteps and errors on the far left. Lenin, himself, mocks what the Russian leader called the ultra-left in his famous *Left-Wing Communism: An Infantile Disorder*. Writing in 1920, the leader of the Bolsheviks asks why things in Germany have gone so badly for the revolutionaries. His answer is, "one of the reasons was the mistaken tactics of the German Communists, who must fearlessly and honestly admit this mistake and learn to rectify it. The mistake lay in their repudiation of the necessity of participating in the reactionary bourgeois parliaments and in the reactionary trade unions."[2] Revolutionaries becoming involved in the bitter and hopeless Berlin street fighting of January 1919 and proceeding to take up power in a clearly impossible situation in Munich that same year are examples of costly far left blunders.

Although right-wing extremism is better known, it demands to be reemphasized. Germany, up to World War I, had seldom before seen such joyful viciousness, brutality and blood lust. Deference towards women gave way to a loathing of females as the incarnation of treasonous evil. Consider the following boast from a *Freikorp* officer who fought the left in 1920. This uniformed butcher participated in sexually charged torture and proudly reported: "We even shot ten Red Cross nurses ... We shot these little ladies with pleasure—how they cried and pleaded with us to save their lives. Nothing doing!"[3]

It is far from unusual to note complications within the far left and few observers can ignore the fierce ruthlessness of the far right. What is more uncommon is understanding, what Tariq Ali in a different context called, the callousness of the extreme center.[4] The right-wing of German Social Democracy easily deserves to be characterized as an example of the extreme center. Although they preached moderation, the SPD leaders showed little restraint in dealing with enemies on the left. Instead, they were completely ruthless in suppressing their leftist opponents. They did not have scruples about using officers from the old Imperial Army and the *Freikorps*, forerunners to the Nazis, even after both proved their disloyalty to any form of parliamentary government.

It was not enough for the SPD to outnumber the USPD and KPD in the Reichstag. Nor was it sufficient to have more supporters than the far left in the trade unions. German Social Democracy refused to trust in the loyalty of their members and supporters. Instead, they turned to the very people who would later overthrow the Weimar Republic. Yes, it was the half-crazed former officers who shot workers and committed atrocities against women. But they did these bloody deeds on the orders of Noske, Ebert, Scheidemann and other leaders of the SPD who failed to rein in these butchers even when innocents were murdered. The men who founded the first German Republic are habitually described, by historians, as moderates. In reality, they were extremists, extremists of the center who would unleash mass carnage so they could continue in their so-called moderation. The SPD led government knew their troops were committing violent atrocities like bayoneting to death prisoners as well as murdering women and children. They "took few measures to constrain their behavior ... [and instead defended] the conduct of government soldiers."[5] If this is not extremism, it is difficult to know what it would be called.

For those who think wisdom lies in the center, this may be hard to accept. Still, how can one understand the huge human cost of a defense of moderation that rested not on the mobilization of large sections of the populace but rather on the guns of proto-fascists if we do not call it by its true name? It should be acknowledged that the gentlefolk of the SPD, who wrapped themselves in the title moderate like people wear heavy coats to ward off cold in winter, were violent extremists … of the center.

Another lesson one must not forget is that the revolution demonstrated how much the common people, and especially women, are a force of history. Neither the exit of Germany from the war nor overthrow of the old monarch was preordained. Both acts were the work of the people in motion. The ordinary people faced clever capitalists who repeatedly pulled their system back from the brink of total collapse. There is little doubt that the leaders of the great capitalist enterprises knew where their self-interest rested. One might say the German upper class was as class conscious as the most politicized worker. In her first speech as a member of the Reichstag, Toni Sender attacked Hugo Stinnes, powerful master of trusts who also had been elected to the German parliament. Stinnes had not bothered to show up and choose instead to negotiate deals with foreign businessmen at Berlin's Hotel Kaiserhof.[6] The female socialist gave what all admitted was a very good speech while Stinnes made what all admitted was a very good deal of money.

Left authors[7] tend to stress the betrayals of German Social Democracy but typically argue all this could have been prevented with a better (read: Leninist) party organization for the masses of the revolutionary left. It is true that German Social Democracy's organizational structures did not prevent the rise of a man like Friedrich Ebert, the first president of the Weimar Republic. But the Bolshevik organizational structures gave us Joe Stalin. It is with a great deal of justice that Friedrich Ebert has been characterized as the "Stalin of German Social Democracy."[8] This is correct in more ways than one. Both men had much in common such as their pathological hatred of the revolutionary left. It would be as pointless as it would be pedantic to try to guess at which person's policies led to more death and suffering.

When the year 1923 failed to witness a victorious upheaval, no further revolution seemed likely. For some few years, Germany was quiet. Then when the crisis of capitalism returned with a vengeance in 1929, the rulers were willing to share power but this time with the far right Nazis who they hoped to control. The same bourgeoisie that had flattered and cajoled German Social Democracy now saw a better way to increase profits by backing the Nazis, a movement big business knew would smash unions and all political dissent. Big business funded the Nazis. The giants of industry, according to many anti-fascists, including Toni Sender, "are responsible for Germany's descent into barbarism."[9]

What the money men did not know, could not know, was that the Nazis would start a war and then lose it. But, that tragedy rests beyond the scope of this book. Yet in all, an argument can be made that the German Revolution did not fail completely. On the positive side, the revolution destroyed Imperial Germany. Kaiser Wilhelm II was to be the last monarch to rule Germany. Instead, a republic was born that, for all its failings, had the most democratic constitution ever implemented in a major country. For example, women were given the vote, something that only transpired in Italy and France a generation later. Had this situation continued for more than the little over a decade that the republic survived, an argument could be advanced about the successes of the German Revolution.

Yet, crippled from birth by German Social Democracy's reliance on the old military leaders and the proto-Nazi *Freikorps*, the revolution could not even deliver a stable or long-lived republic. The revolution also raised a number of significant issues concerning a socialist transformation. There was the issue of the strengths and weaknesses of Workers' Councils in a revolutionary situation. It was vital for the left to realize that the right had a far greater willingness to use deathly violence. Further, the counter-revolution could not be expected to play by any of "the rules of the game" regardless of their promises. Additionally, after November 1918 aside from Clara Zetkin, much of the left seemed to forget the centrality of women to any revolutionary enterprise. Noticeably, the far-right would almost always have advantages never seen by the far-left since the former had the tacit support of the army and government bureaucracy.

The question remained open as to the type of revolutionary party organization most suited to advanced industrial society. Was a pure and simple Leninist model suitable to an advanced capitalist society with formal political democracy and civil liberties unknown in Czarist Russia? In a 1904 critique of Bolshevism, Rosa Luxemburg thought not: "The working class demands the right to make its mistakes and learn the dialectic of history. Let us speak plainly. Historically, the errors committed by a truly revolutionary movement are infinitely more fruitful than the infallibility of the cleverest Central Committee."[10]

Could any "parliamentary road to socialism" be successful given the absolute commitment of big business and the army to prevent any truly radical transformation? Besides, it must be recognized that developments during a Revolution happen with such rapidity that some level of confusion is to be expected among the people. The revolutionary moment is far more complex than many later authors suggest. Of course, had the German Revolution been radical and purged the old state apparatus, there would most likely have been no Nazi seizure of power, no Third Reich, no World War II, no Holocaust. Unhappily, that opportunity to sweep away the powerful pests of the past was squandered.

It is said that those who make revolutions halfway only dig their own graves. Sadly, this cliché relates more persuasively to the German Revolution of 1918–19 than to most half-finished transformations. Moderation won out, albeit after a mountain of corpses and rivers of blood, and it proved ultimately wanting. Historians have too often contemplated the causes of historical events in the feats and foibles of leaders. In so doing, they deny the agency of ordinary people who, as the German Revolution revealed, have more power than history is accustomed to credit them. The common people make their own history, just not in the conditions they would wish.

Notes

Introduction: What German Revolution?

1. The most infamous is the viciously anti-Semitic *Protocols of the Elders of Zion*. See B. W. Segel and R. S. Levy, *A Lie and a Libel: The History of the Protocols of the Elders of Zion*, Lincoln, NE: University of Nebraska Press, 1995. In addition, there are "secret histories" that claim evidence of civilizations living inside a hollow earth, or welsh-speaking Native Americans. Some claim the pyramids were built by space aliens. The list is, sadly, long.
2. Edward Hallett Carr, *What is History?*, New York: Vintage Books, 1961: 159.
3. The Krupps are historically one of the largest industrial groups in Germany. See William Manchester, *The Arms of Krupp, 1587–1968*, Boston, MA: Little, Brown, 1968.
4. This is a common name that is often used as a synonym for a typical German.
5. Founder of the "Illuminati."
6. Winston S. Churchill, "ZIONISM versus BOLSHEVISM," *Illustrated Sunday Herald* (London), February 8, 1920: 5.
7. Ibid.
8. There is scant evidence that John D. Rockefeller set up the University of Chicago in order to undermine capitalism or that his son Nelson funded failed historian Henry Kissinger to promote radicalism.
9. J. H. Plumb, *The Death of the Past*, New York: Palgrave Macmillan, 2004: 40.
10. A. J. P. Taylor, *From Napoleon to Stalin*, London: Hamish Hamilton, 1950: 74.

11. Robert F. Wheeler, "'Ex oriente lux?' The Soviet example and the German Revolution, 1917–1923," in Charles L. Bertrand (ed.), *Revolutionary Situations in Europe, 1917–1922: Germany, Italy Austria-Hungary*, Montreal: Interuniversity Centre for European Studies, 1977: 39.

12. Reinhard Rürup, "Problems of the German Revolution 1918–1919," *Journal of Contemporary History*, 3(4), October 1968: 110.

13. This extended to some leftist scholars in the West. See Eric Hobsbawm, "Confronting defeat: The German Communist Party," *New Left Review*, 61, 1970: 83–92.

14. See, for example, Rob Sewell, *Germany: From Revolution to Counter-Revolution*, London: Wellred Books, 2014.

15. Chris Harman, *The Lost Revolution: Germany 1918–1923*, London: Bookmarks, 1997: 86.

16. Eric D. Weitz, *Weimar Germany: Promise and Tragedy*, Princeton, NJ: Princeton University Press, 2007: 39.

1. Industrialization and the Emergence of the German Working Class

1. Frederick Engels, *Germany: Revolution and Counter Revolution*, edited by Eleanor Marx, New York: International Publishers, 1969: 12.

2. See the broader definition contained in Marcel van der Linden, *Workers of the World*, Leiden: Brill Academic Publishing, 2010.

3. Alfred Kelly (ed.), *The German Worker: Working-Class Autobiographies from the Age of Industrialization*, Berkeley, CA: University of California Press, 1987: 143.

4. Ibid.: 363.

5. Ibid.: 255.

6. Gertrud Hanna, "Women in the German trade union movement," *International Labour Review*, VIII, July 1923: 26.

7. Kelly, *The German Worker*: 259.
8. Frau Dr Minna Wettstein-Adelt, *3½ Monate Fabrik-Arbeiterin*, Berlin: J. Leiser, 1893: 25–6.
9. Edward Ross Dickinson, Sex, Freedom and Power in Imperial Germany, 1880–1914, New York: Cambridge University Press, 2014: 142. See also, William A. Pelz, *Against Capitalism: The European Left on the March*, New York: Peter Lang, 2007: 25.
10. Kelly, *The German Worker*: 79.
11. Ibid.
12. Ibid.: 84.
13. Ibid.: 193.
14. Ibid.: 401.
15. Ibid.: 403–4.
16. Ibid.: 405.
17. Anthony Oberschall, *Empirical Social Research in Germany, 1848–1914*, New York: Basic Books, 1965: 71.
18. Sophie Twarog, "Heights and living standards in Germany, 1850–1939," in Richard H. Steckel and Roderick Floud (eds.), *Health and Welfare during Industrialization*, Chicago, IL: University of Chicago Press, 1997: 315.
19. Ibid.: 318.
20. Kelly, *The German Worker*: 271–2.
21. Ibid.: 273.
22. Oberschall, *Empirical Social Research in Germany, 1848–1914*: 122.
23. Harry J. Marks, "The sources of reformism in the Social Democratic Party of Germany, 1890–1914," *Journal of Modern History*, XI(3), September 1939: 334–56.
24. Richard J. Evans, "Proletarian mentalities: Pub conversations in Hamburg," in his *Proletarians and Politics: Socialism, Protest, and the Working Class in Germany before the First World War*, New York: St. Martin's Press, 1990.
25. Kelly, *The German Worker*: 28.
26. Ibid.: 29.

27. Ludwig Weber, "Wohnungen und Sonntagsbeschäftigung der deutschen Arbeiter: Nach urkundlichen Quellen geschildert," *Sammlung theologischer und sozialer Reden und Abhandlungen*, III(8/9), Leipzig, 1892: 212–13.

28. Ibid.

29. Twarog, "Heights and living standards in Germany, 1850–1939": 320.

30. Wilhelm Reich, "The sexual misery of the working masses and the difficulties of sexual reform," *New German Critique*, 1, Winter 1973: 98–110.

31. Twarog, "Heights and living standards in Germany, 1850–1939": 317.

32. James S. Roberts, "Drink and the Labour Movement: The Schaps boycott of 1909," in Richard J. Evans (ed.), *The German Working Class, 1888–1933*, London: Croom Helm, 1982: 102.

33. Ibid.: 103.

34. Michael Grüttner, "Working-class crime and the Labour Movement: Pilfering in the Hamburg docks, 1888–1923" in Richard J. Evans, *The German Working Class, 1888–1933*, London: Croom Helm, 1982: 65.

35. Halvor Mehlum, Edward Miguel and Ragnar Torvik, "Poverty and crime in 19th century Germany," *Journal of Urban Economics*, 59, 2006: 370–88.

36. Christain Traxler and Carsten Burhop, *Poverty and Crime in 19th Century Germany: A Reassessment*, Bonn: Max Planck Institute for Research on Collective Goods, 2010: 14.

37. Johann Wolfgang von Goethe, "Ein Andres," retrieved on February 19, 2018 from https://copticliterature.wordpress.com/2012/06/14/goethes-other-coptic-song-ein-andres.

2.   *The Rise of Popular Radicalism*

1. At this point, there is little point in being sidetracked into the seemingly endless debate, so often engaged in by intellectuals, about what "socialism" really means.

2. *Social-Demokrat*, September 21, 1870.

3. William H. Maehl, *August Bebel, Shadow Emperor of the German Workers*, Philadelphia, PA: American Philosophical Society, 1980.

4. August Bebel, *Aus meinem Leben*, vol. 11, Berlin: Dietz Verlag, 1953: 182.

5. Karl Marx and Frederick Engels, *Collected Works*, vol. 24, New York: International Publishers, 1989: 75–99.

6. Franz Osterroth and Dieter Schuster, *Chronik der deutschen Sozialdemokratie*, vol. 1, Berlin: Dietz Verlag, 1975: 53.

7. C. J. H. Hayes, "The history of German socialism reconsidered," *American History Review* XXIII (1), 1917: 74.

8. Osterroth and Schuster, *Chronik der deutchen Sozialdemokratie*: 70.

9. Vernon L. Lidtke, *The Outlawed Part: Social Democracy in Germany, 1878–1890*, Princeton, NJ: Princeton University Press, 1966: 96.

10. Osterroth and Schuster, *Chronik der deutchen Sozialdemokratie*: 70.

11. Alfred Kelly (ed.), *The German Worker: Working-Class Autobiographies from the Age of Industrialization*, Berkeley, CA: University of California Press, 1987: 263.

12. Mary Jo Maynes, *Taking the Hard Road: Life Course in the French and German Workers Autobiographies in the Era of Industrialization*, Chapel Hill, NC: University of North Carolina Press, 1995: 4–6.

13. Peter Gay, *The Dilemma off Democratic Socialism*, New York: Columbia University Press, 1952 is the standard English language biography of Bernstein and his theories.

14. Lidtke, *The Outlawed Part*: 234.

15. Hayes, "The history of German socialism reconsidered": 81.

16. Toni Sender, *The Autobiography of a German Rebel*, New York: Vanguard Press, 1939: 28.

17. Richard Critchfield, "Toni Sender: feminist, socialist, internationalist," *History of European Ideas*, 15(4–6), 1992: 701–6.

18. Ruth Fischer, *Stalin and German Communism*, Cambridge, MA: Harvard University Press, 1948: 4.
19. A groundbreaking work on this topic is Vernon L. Lidtke, *The Alternative Culture: Socialist Labor in Imperial Germany*, New York: Oxford University Press, 1985.
20. In addition to Lidtke, see Gary P. Steenson, *After Marx, Before Lenin: Marxism and Socialist Working-Class Parties in Europe, 1884–1914*, Pittsburgh, PA: University of Pittsburgh Press, 1991.
21. Hans-Josef Steinberg and Nicholas Jacobs, "Workers' libraries in Germany before 1914," *History Workshop*, 1, Spring 1978: 166–80.
22. Robert F. Wheeler, "Organized sport and organized labour: The workers' sports movement," *Journal of Contemporary History*, 13(2), 1978: 191–210.
23. Michael Krüger, "The German workers' sport movement between socialism, workers' culture, middle-class gymnastics and sport for all," *The International Journal of the History of Sport*, 31(9), 2014: 1098–1117.
24. Lynn Abrams, *Workers' Culture in Imperial Germany: Leisure and Recreation in the Rhineland and Westphalia*, London: Routledge, 1992: 116–17.
25. Lidtke, *The Alternative Culture:* 74.
26. V. I. Lenin, "The Balkan War and bourgeois chauvinism," in *Collected Works*, vol. 19, Moscow: Progress Publishers, 1977: 39–40.
27. V. I. Lenin. "The development of workers' choirs in Germany," in *Collected Works*, vol. 36, Moscow: Progress Publishers, 1971: 225–6.
28. Lidtke, *The Alternative Culture:* 191.
29. Richard J. Evans, *Death in Hamburg, Society and Politics in the Cholera Years*, New York: Penguin Books, 1987: 94–5.
30. Gary D. Stark, *Banned in Berlin: Literary Censorship in Imperial Germany, 1871–1918*, New York: Berghahn Books, 2009: 132.

31. *Andrew Bonnell, The People's Stage in Imperial Germany: Social Democracy and Culture 1890–1914, London:* I. B. Tauris, 2005.

32. Stark, *Banned in Berlin*: 132–3.

33. Maynes, *Taking the Hard Road*: 162.

34. Andrew G. Bonnell, "Did they read Marx? Marx reception and Social Democratic members in Imperial Germany," *Australian Journal of Politics and History*, 48(1), 2002: 4–15.

35. Kelly, *The German Worker*: 44.

36. Ibid.: 45.

37. Ibid.: 394–5.

38. Ibid.: 395–6.

39. Jürgen Kuczynski, *A Short History of Labour Conditions under Industrial Capitalism, Vol. 3, Part I: Germany to the Present Day*, London: Frederick Muller, 1945: 141.

40. Richard W. Reichard, "The German working class and the Russian Revolution of 1905," *Journal of Central European Affairs*, XIII, 1953: 136–53.

41. Ibid.: 143.

42. Gustav Stengele, "Der 17. Januar in Hamburg," *Die Neue Zeit*, XXIV(1), 1905/6: 620.

43. Reichard, "The German working class and the Russian Revolution of 1905": 145.

44. Oberschall, *Empirical Social Research in Germany, 1848–1914*: 95.

45. Ibid.: 105.

46. Ibid..

47. Ibid.: 106.

48. William A. Pelz, *A People's History of Modern Europe*, London: Pluto Press, 2016: 104–6.

49. Julius Koettgen, *A German Deserter's War Experience: Fighting for the Kaiser in the First World War*, Barnsley: Pen & Sword, 2013: 11.

50. Jeffrey Verhey, *The Spirit of 1914: Militarism, Myth and Mobilization in Germany*, Cambridge: Cambridge University Press, 2000: 52–7.
51. Ottokar Luban, "Rosa Luxemburg's fight for peace," paper presented to Luxemburg Conference in Johannesburg, South Africa, May 20–22, 2004: 4.

3. War, Suffering and Resistance

1. Oliver Janz, *14–Der Grosse Krieg*, Frankfurt: Campus Verlag, 2013.
2. J. Jemnitz, *The Danger of War and the Second International*, trans. P. Félix, Budapest: Akadémiai Kiadó, 1972 [1911].
3. For more on the German rural population, see: Frank B. Tipton, "Farm labor and power politics: Germany, 1850–1914," *The Journal of Economic History*, 34(4), December 1974: 951–79.
4. Ebba Dahlin, *French and German Public Opinion on Declared War Aims, 1914–1918*, Oxford: Oxford University Press, 1933: 18.
5. Jeffrey Verhey, *The Spirit of 1914: Militarism, Myth and Mobilization in Germany*, Cambridge: Cambridge University Press, 2000: 167.
6. Dahlin, *French and German Public Opinion*: 26.
7. Karl Liebknecht, *The Future Belongs to the People*, New York: The Macmillan Company, 1918: 31–3.
8. Lawrence Sondhaus, *World War One: The Global Revolution*, Cambridge: Cambridge University Press, 2011: 206.
9. William Hermanns, *The Holocaust: From a Survivor of Verdun*, New York: Harper & Row, 1972: 61.
10. Ibid.: 64.
11. Richard Van Emden, *Meeting the Enemy: The Human Face of the Great War*, London: Bloomsbury, 2013: 134.
12. Ernst Toller, *I was a German: The Autobiography of a Revolutionary*, New York: Paragon House, 1991: 62.

13. Richard Stumpf, *War, Mutiny and Revolution in the Germany Navy: The World War I Diary of Seaman Richard Stumpf,* ed. Daniel Horn, New Brunswick, NJ: Rutgers University Press, 1967: 43.

14. Dahlin, *French and German Public Opinion*: 31.

15. Ute Lischke, *Lily Braun, 1865–1916: German Writer, Feminist, Socialist,* Rochester, NY: Camden House, 2000: 114.

16. Hermann Duncker and Käte Duncker, *Ein Tagebuch in Briefen (1894–1953),* Berlin: Dietz Verlag, 2016.

17. Werner Thönnessen, *The Emancipation of Women: The Rise and Decline of the Women's Movement in German Social Democracy, 1863–1933,* London: Pluto Press, 1973: 75–6.

18. Clara Zetkin, *Selected Writings,* ed. Philip S. Foner, Chicago, IL: Haymarket Books, 2015: 112.

19. Belinda J. Davis, *Home Fires Burning: Food, Politics and Everyday Life in World War I Berlin,* Chapel Hill, NC: University of North Carolina Press, 2000: 24–5.

20. Susan R. Grayzel, *The First World War: A Brief History with Documents,* Boston, MA: Bedford/St. Martin's, 2013: 94.

21. "Bread riots in Germany," *Dominion,* 8(2395), February 26, 1915: 1.

22. Robert G. Moeller, "Dimensions of social conflict in the Great War: The view from the German countryside," *Central European History,* XIV(2), June 1981: 168.

23. Toni Sender, *The Autobiography of a German Rebel,* New York: Vanguard Press, 1939: 62.

24. Ibid.: 63.

25. Toller, *I was a German*: 82.

26. Fritz Kreisler, *Four Weeks in the Trenches,* Boston, MA: Houghton Mifflin Company, 1915: 76.

27. Koettgen, *A German Deserter's War Experience*: 68–9.

28. Ibid.: 70–71.

29. A. E. Ashworth, "The sociology of trench warfare 1914–18," *The British Journal of Sociology,* 19(4), December 1968: 408.

30. Tony Ashworth, *Trench Warfare 1914–18: The Live and Let Live System*, London: Pan, 2004.

31. Ashworth, "The sociology of trench warfare 1914–18": 421.

32. Emily Brewer, *Tommy, Doughboy, Fritz: Soldier Slang of World War I*, Gloucestershire (UK): Amberley Publishing, 2014: 199.

33. Ibid.: 192.

34. Ibid.: 211.

35. Marc Ferro, Malcolm Brown, Rémy Cazals and Olaf Mueller, *Meetings in No Man's Land, Christmas 1914 and Fraternization in the Great War*, London: Constable & Robinson, 2007.

36. Van Emden, *Meeting the Enemy*: 80.

37. Stanley Weintraub, *Silent Night: The Story of the World War I Christmas Truce*, New York: Penguin Books, 2002: 28.

38. Van Emden, *Meeting the Enemy*: 83.

39. Malcolm Brown and Shirley Seaton, *Christmas Truce: the Western Front December 1914*, London: Pan Books, 1994: 163.

40. Ibid.: xxi.

41. Ibid.: 196–206.

42. John Huston, *Christmas 1914: The First World War at Home and Abroad*, Stroud, 2014: 242.

43. Ashworth, *Trench Warfare 1914–18*: 102.

44. Ibid.: 140.

45. *Norddeutche Allgemeine Zeitung*, March 4, 1915.

46. Ralph Haswell Lutz (ed.), *The Causes of the German Collapse in 1918*, New York: Archon Books, 1969: 183.

47. Ibid.: 186.

48. "Government control of food supplies in Germany," *Monthly Review of the US Bureau of Labor Statistics*, 4(5), May 1917: 724.

49. Grayzel, *The First World War*: 95.

50. Evelyn, Princess Blücher, *An English Wife in Berlin*, New York: E. P. Dutton & Company, 1920: 95.

51. Hermanns, *The Holocaust*: 73.

52. John Williams, *The Other Battlefield: The Home Fronts: Britain, France and Germany, 1914–1918* Chicago: Henry Regnery Company, 1972:157–158.
53. Ibid.: 156.
54. Ibid.: 225.
55. Sender, *Autobiography of a German Rebel*: 91.
56. Zetkin, *Selected Writings*: 130.
57. James W. Gerard, *My Four Years in Germany*, New York: Grosset and Dunlap Publishers, 1917: 295.
58. Evelyn, Princess Blücher, *An English Wife in Berlin*: 90–91.
59. Sender, *Autobiography of a German Rebel*: 75.
60. Gerald D. Feldman, *Army, Industry, and Labor in Germany, 1914–1918*, Princeton, NJ: Princeton University Press, 1966: 469.
61. Rosa Luxemburg, *Gesamelte Werke*, vol. 4, Berlin: Dietz Verlag, 1979: 163.
62. Sondhaus, *World War One*: 210.
63. Ibid.: 216.
64. Philipp Witkop (ed.), *German Students' War Letters*, Philadelphia, PA: University of Pennsylvania Press, 2002: 228.
65. Stumpf, *War, Mutiny and Revolution in the Germany Navy*: 174.
66. Ibid.: 176.
67. Ottokar Luban, "Rosa Luxemburg and the revolutionary antiwar mass strikes in Germany during World War I," paper presented to A Century+ of May Day, DePaul University, Chicago, IL, April 30–May 2, 2010: 4.
68. Karl Liebkncht, *Gesammelte Reden und Schriften*, vol. VIII, Berlin: Dietz Verlag, 1974: 613–16. For an account of this entire episode, see the Spartakus report entitled "Die Maifier" in Institut für Marxismus-Leninismus, *Dokumente und Materialien zur Geschichte der Deutschen Arbeiterbewegung*, vol. I, Reihle II Berlin: Dietz Verlag, 1958: 376–8.
69. Verhey, *The Spirit of 1914*: 167.
70. *Vorwärts*, January 1, 1917.

71. Witkop, *German Students' War Letters*: 198.
72. Ibid.: 199.
73. Ibid.: 205.

4.   The Road to the November Revolution

1. Paul Lerner, "Psychiatry and casualties of war in Germany, 1914–18," *Journal of Contemporary History*, 35(1), January 2000: 18.
2. Ibid.: 27.
3. Erich Maria Remarque, *All Quiet on the Western Front*, New York: Ballantine Books, 1958: 293.
4. Mary Ethel McAuley, *Germany in War Time*, Chicago, IL: The Open Court Publishing Co., 1917: 59.
5. Ute Daniel, *The War Within: German Working Class Women in the First World War*, New York: Berg, 1997: 285.
6. David Khoudour-Castéras, "Welfare state and labor mobility: The impact of Bismarck's social legislation on German emigration before World War I," *The Journal of Economic History*, 68(1), March 2008: 211–43.
7. Jeffrey Verhey, *The Spirit of 1914: Militarism, Myth and Mobilization in Germany*, Cambridge: Cambridge University Press, 2000: 56.
8. Ibid.: 57.
9. Ibid.: 91.
10. Ibid.: 88.
11. Ibid.: 89.
12. A brilliant new and definitive treatment of this group is Ralf Hoffrogge, *Working Class Politics in the German Revolution: Richard Müller, the Revolutionary Shop Stewards and the Origins of the Council Movement*, Chicago, IL: Haymarket Books, 2015.
13. Icarus (Ernst Scheider), *The Wilhelmshaven Revolt: A Chapter of the Revolutionary Movement in the German Navy 1918–1919*, Honley: Simian Press, 1975.

14. Carl E. Schorske, *German Social Democracy 1905–1917: The Development of the Great Schism*, Cambridge, MA: Harvard University Press, 1955.

15. Hans Kollwitz (ed.), *The Diary and letters of Käthe Kollwitz*, Evanston, IL: Northwestern University Press, 1988: 155.

16. Evelyn, Princess Blücher, *An English Wife in Berlin*, New York: E. P. Dutton & Company, 1920: 176.

17. Hoffrogge, *Working Class Politics in the German Revolution*: 40–42.

18. Ottokar Luban, "Rosa Luxemburg and the revolutionary antiwar mass strikes in Germany during World War I," paper presented to A Century+ of May Day, DePaul University, Chicago, IL, April 30–May 2, 2010: 5.

19. Friedhelm Boll, "Spontaneität der Basis und Politische Funktion des Streiks 1914–1918: Das Beispiel Braunschweig," *Archiv für Sozialgeschichte*, 17, 1977: 354–55.

20. Pierre Broué, *The German Revolution, 1917–1923*, Chicago, IL: Haymarket Books, 2006: 100.

21. Theodor Plivier, *The Kaiser's Coolies*, New York: Alfred A. Knopf, 1931: 280–81.

22. Daniel Horn, *The German Naval Mutinies of World War I*, New Brunswick, NJ: Rutgers University Press, 1969: 136–7.

23. Richard Stumpf, *War, Mutiny and Revolution in the Germany Navy: The World War I Diary of Seaman Richard Stumpf*, ed. Daniel Horn, New Brunswick, NJ: Rutgers University Press, 1967: 374. For more on this remarkable sailor, see Daniel Horn, "The diarist revisited: the papers of Seaman Stumpf," *Journal of the Rutgers University Library*, 40 (1): 32–48.

24. Stumpf, *War, Mutiny and Revolution in the Germany Navy*: 346–7.

25. Ibid.: 348.

26. Russia still used an archaic calendar so that the "February Revolution" took place in March and "October Revolution"

happened in November according to the calendar used in the Western world.

27. Leon Trotsky, *History of the Russian Revolution*, Chicago, IL: Haymarket Books, 2017.

28. Tariq Ali, *The Dilemmas of Lenin: Terrorism, War, Empire, Love, Revolution*, London: Verso, 2017: 190.

29. Toni Sender, *The Autobiography of a German Rebel*, New York: Vanguard Press, 1939: 96.

30. Broué, *The German Revolution, 1917–1923*: 120.

31. Clara Zetkin, *Selected Writings*, ed. Philip S. Foner, Chicago, IL: Haymarket Books, 2015: 141.

32. George G. Bruntz, "Allied propaganda and the collapse of German morale in 1918," *The Public Opinion Quarterly*, 2(1), January, 1938: 61–76.

33. Ibid.: 71.

34. Ibid.: 72.

35. Field Marshal von Hindernburg, *The Great War*, London: Greenhill Books, 2006: 203.

36. Gerald D. Feldman, "The social and economic policies of German big business, 1918–1929," *The American Historical Review*, 75(1), October 1969: 47.

37. Ibid.: 48.

38. Schorske, *German Social Democracy 1905–1917*: 322.

39. Maximillian, Prince of Baden, *The Memoirs of Prince Max of Baden*, vol. II, New York: Charles Scribner's Sons, 1928: 312.

40. Ottokar Luban, "Rosa Luxemburg's fight for peace," paper presented to Luxemburg Conference in Johannesburg, South Africa, May 20–22, 2004: 5.

41. Ottokar Luban, "Together with Rosa Luxemburg for peace, social justice and revolution (August 1914–November 1918): The female German Spartacus militants Clara Zetkin, Käte Duncker, Mathilde Jacob, Fanny Jezierska, Berta Thalheimer," paper presented to the Historical Materialism Conference, London, November, 2016.

42. Hoffrogge, *Working Class Politics in the German Revolution*: 29.
43. Ibid.: 30.
44. Ibid.: 31.
45. Ibid.: 108–17.
46. Ibid.: 79.
47. Alexander Watson, *Ring of Steel: Germany and Austria-Hungary in World War I*, New York: Basic Books, 2014: 495.
48. Hoffrogge, *Working Class Politics in the German Revolution*: 49.
49. *Vorwärts*, January 29, 1918: 1.
50. Arthur Rosenberg, *The Birth of the German Republic*, New York: Russel & Russell, 1962: 211.
51. *Vorwärts*, January 29, 1918: 1.
52. Rosenberg, *The Birth of the German Republic*: 215–16.
53. Hoffrogge, *Working Class Politics in the German Revolution*: 56.
54. Ottokar Luban, "Zwei Schreiben der Spartakus-Zentrale an Rosa Luxemburg," *Archiv für Sozialgeschichte*, 11 (1971): 225–40.
55. Hoffrogge, *Working Class Politics in the German Revolution*: 49–56.
56. For a detailed examination of the power struggles within the naval commands' upper echelons and the mutinies of 1918, see Wilhelm Deist, "Die Politik der Seekriegsleitung und die Rebellion der Flotte Ende Oktober 1918," *Vierteljahrshefte für Zeitgeschichte*, 14(4), 1966: 341–68.
57. Horn, *The German Naval Mutinies of World War I*: 203–5.
58. Ibid.: 206.
59. Ibid.: 216.
60. Ibid.: 220–21.
61. Stumpf, *War, Mutiny and Revolution in the Germany Navy*: 417–20.
62. Icarus (Ernst Scheider), *The Wilhelmshaven Revolt: A Chapter of the Revolutionary Movement in the German Navy*

1918–1919, Honley: Simian Press, 1975: 17. Karl Liebknecht had become a symbol of opposition to the war by this time.

63. Horn, *The German Naval Mutinies of World War I*: 225–226.

64. For a brief popular account of the events that followed, see David Woodward, "Mutiny at Kiel, 1918," *History Today*, 18(12): 829–35.

65. Karl Artelt, "With the red flag to Vice-Admiral Souchon," in Gabriel Kuhn (ed.), *All Power to the Councils: A Documentary History of the German Revolution of 1918–1919*, Oakland, CA: PM Press, 2012: 19–24.

66. Broué, *The German Revolution, 1917–1923*: 139–40.

67. Artelt, "With the red flag to Vice-Admiral Souchon": 22.

68. For a sympathetic biography take note of Ulrich Czisnik, *Gustav Noske: Ein sozialdemokratischer staats-mann*, Göttingen: Musterschmidt Verlag, 1969.

69. David Woodward, *The Collapse of Power: Mutiny in the High Sea Fleet*, London: Arthur Barker, 1973: 148–150.

70. Stumpf, *War, Mutiny and Revolution in the Germany Navy*: 426.

71. Richard A. Comfort, *Revolutionary Hamburg: Labor Politics in the Early Weimar Republic*, Stanford, CA: Stanford University Press, 1966: 36.

72. For a fuller discussion of the revolution in Bremen, consult Peter Kuckuck (ed.), *Revolution and Raterepublick in Bremen*, Frankfurt: Suhrkamp Verlag, 1969.

73. One useful introduction in English is Allen Mitchell, *Revolution in Bavaria 1918–1919: The Eisner Regime and the Soviet Republic*, Princeton, NJ: Princeton University Press, 1965. A more popularly written and not very academic account is Richard Grunberger, *Red Rising in Bavaria*, London: Arthur Barker, 1973.

74. In order to gain some understanding of this very complex man, one would do well to consult his writings. One excellent collection is Kurt Eisner, *Die halbe Macht den Räten: Aus-*

gewählte Aufsätze und Reden, edited by Renata and Gerhard Schmolze, Cologne: Verlag Jakob Hegner, 1969.

75. Note Eisner's Proclamation of the Republic in Gerhard Ritter and Susanne Miller (ed.), *Die deutsche Revolution 1918–1919: Dokumente*, Hamburg: Hoffmann und Came Verlag, 1975: 61–2, and Eisner's article "Revolutionsfeier" in his *Die halbe Macht den Räten*, 277–80. For a study of the church's role during the revolution, see Ludwig Hüttl, "Die Stellungnahme der katholische Kirche und Publizistik zur Revolution in Bayern 1918/19," *Zeitschrift für Bayerische Landesgeschichte*, 34(2), 1971: 652–92.

76. One detailed regional study of this area is Ulrich Kluge, "Das 'württembergische Volksheer' 1918–1919: Zum Problem der bewaffneten Macht in der deutschen Revolution," in *Klassenjustiz und Pluralismus: Festcshrift für Ernst Fraenkel zum Geburtstag*, Hamburg: Hoffmann & Campe Verlag, 1973: 92–130.

77. Feldman, "The social and economic policies of German big business, 1918–1929": 49.

78. Maximillian, Prince of Baden, *The Memoirs of Prince Max of Baden*, vol. II: 301.

79. Wolfgang J. Mommsen, "Kaiser Wilhelm II and German politics," *Journal of Contemporary History*, 28(2/3), June 1990: 313.

5. *The Kaiser Goes, the Generals Remain*

1. An important correction is Mark Jones, *Founding Weimar: Violence and the German Revolution of 1918–1919*, Cambridge: Cambridge University Press, 2016.

2. They were killed on January 15, 1919, as all historians now agree.

3. Erick Eyck, *A History of the Weimar Republic*, vol. I, New York: Atheneum, 1970: 53 (emphasis added).

4. Leon Trotsky, History of the Russian Revolution, Chicago, IL: Haymarket Books, 2017: 414.

5. Dick Geary, "Identifying militancy: The assessment of working class attitudes towards state and society," in Richard J. Evans (ed.), *The German Working Class, 1888–1933*, London: Croom Helm, 1982: 222.

6. V. I. Lenin, *Collected Works*, vol. 27, Moscow: Progress Publishers, 1965: 98–9.

7. William T. Ham, "Labor under the German Empire," *The Quarterly Journal of Economics*, 48(2), February 1934: 206.

8. Richard A. Comfort, *Revolutionary Hamburg: Labor Politics in the Early Weimar Republic*, Stanford, CA: Stanford University Press, 1966: 35–9.

9. Ibid.: 42–3.

10. Ibid.: 57.

11. Ibid.: 58.

12. Toni Sender, *The Autobiography of a German Rebel*, New York: Vanguard Press, 1939: 98.

13. Ibid.: 111.

14. Leon Trotsky, cited in "The police and 1918–19 German Revolution," *Spartacist*, 65, Summer 2017: 30.

15. Gerhard Engel, "The international communists of Germany, 1916–1919," in Ralf Hoffrogge and Norman LaPorte, *Weimar Communism as Mass Movement, 1918–1933*, London: Lawrence & Wishart, 2017.

16. John Gerber, "From left radicalism to council communism: Anton Pannekoek and German revolutionary Marxism," *Journal of Contemporary History*, 23(2), April 1988: 180.

17. Pierre Broué, *The German Revolution, 1917–1923*, Chicago, IL: Haymarket Books, 2006: 142–3.

18. Ernst Toller, *I was a German: The Autobiography of a Revolutionary*, New York: Paragon House, 1991: 143–4.

19. Victor Klemperer, *Munich 1919: Diary of a Revolution*, Cambridge: Polity Press, 2017: 27.

20. Paul Portner, "The writers' revolution: Munich 1918–19," *Journal of Contemporary History*, 3(4), October 1968: 137–51.

21. Klemperer, *Munich 1919*: 28.

22. John Riddell, *The German Revolution and the Debate on Soviet Power*, New York: Pathfinder Press, 1986: 222–4.

23. Tammy M. Proctor, *Civilians in a World at War, 1914–1918*, New York: NYU Press, 2010: 252.

24. Eric D. Weitz, *Creating German Communism, 1890–1990: From Popular Protest to Socialist State*, Princeton, NJ: Princeton University Press, 1997: 87.

25. Ute Daniel, *The War Within: German Working Class Women in the First World War*, New York: Berg, 1997: 292.

26. Ibid.: 293

27. Jones, *Founding Weimar*: 24.

28. Ibid.: 25.

29. Hermann Duncker and Käte Duncker, *Ein Tagebuch in Briefen (1894–1953)*, Berlin: Dietz Verlag, 2016: 3044.

30. Ebert's role during the revolution is discussed with reference to this point in D. K. Buse, "Ebert and the German crisis 1917–1920," *Central European History*, 5(3), 1972: 234–55.

31. "Aufruf des Vorstandes der SPD vom 4. November 1918," in Institut für Marxismus-Leninismus (ed.), *Dokumenteund Materialien zur Geschichte der deutschen Arbeiterbewegung, Reihe II (1914–1945)*, vol. 2, Berlin: Dietz Verlag, 1957: 289–90.

32. Kaiser Wilhelm II, *The Kaiser's Memoirs*, New York: Harper & Brothers Publishers, 1922: 340.

33. Maximillian, Prince of Baden, *The Memoirs of Prince Max of Baden*, vol. II, New York: Charles Scribner's Sons, 1928: 313.

34. Jones, *Founding Weimar*: 55.

35. Peter Hans Hanssen, *Diary of a Dying Empire*, Bloomington, IN: Indiana University Press, 1955: 350.

36. Philipp Scheidemann, *Memorien eines Sozialdemokraten*, Dresden: Carl Reissner, 1930: 310–312.

NOTES

37. Ibid.: 313.
38. For another view of this event, see Hanssen, *Diary of a Dying Empire*: 351–2. Hanssen had the dubious distinction of being the man who held Scheidemann's feet as the Social Democrat leaned over the balcony to address the crowd.
39. Emil Barth, *Aus der Werkstatt der deutschen Revolution*, Berlin: A. Hoffman's Verlag, 1919: 58–9.
40. Hanssen, *Diary of a Dying Empire*: 360.
41. Mark Jones, "The crowd in the German November Revolution," in Klaus Weinhauer, Anthony McElligott and Kirsten Heinsohn (eds.), *Germany 1916–23: A Revolution in Context*, Bielefeld: Transcript Verlag, 2015.
42. Evelyn, Princess Blücher, *An English Wife in Berlin*, New York: E. P. Dutton & Company, 1920: 279.
43. Ibid.: 280.
44. Such prejudices against crowds are typical of the upper classes, see George Rudé, *The Crowd in History*, New York: Wiley & Sons, 1964.
45. Jones, *Founding Weimar*: 90.
46. Kathleen Canning, "Gender and the imaginary of revolution in Germany," in Klaus Weinhauer, Anthony McElligott and Kirsten Heinsohn (eds.), *Germany 1916–23: A Revolution in Context*, Bielefeld: Transcript Verlag, 2015: 112.
47. Moabit penitentiary was constructed in 1849.
48. See Ottokar Luban, "Together with Rosa Luxemburg for peace, social justice and revolution (August 1914–November 1918): The female German Spartacus militants Clara Zetkin, Käte Duncker, Mathilde Jacob, Fanny Jezierska, Berta Thalheimer," paper presented to the Historical Materialism Conference, London, November, 2016.
49. Duncker and Duncker, *Ein Tagebuch in Briefen (1894–1953)*: 3056.
50. Ralf Hoffrogge, *Working Class Politics in the German Revolution: Richard Müller, the Revolutionary Shop Stewards*

and the Origins of the Council Movement, Chicago, IL: Haymarket Books, 2015: 74.

51. There were no women among the six People's Deputies. The "People's Deputies" are translated as "People's Commissars" in some English-language accounts.

52. Hoffrogge, *Working Class Politics in the German Revolution*: 80–83.

53. For a view from the leadership of the Revolutionary Shop Stewards see Richard Müller, "Democracy or dictatorship," in Gabriel Kuhn (ed.), *All Power to the Councils: A Documentary History of the German Revolution of 1918–1919*, Oakland, CA: PM Press, 2012: 59–75.

54. Hoffrogge, *Working Class Politics in the German Revolution*: 84.

55. Müller, "Democracy or dictatorship": 73–4.

56. Rosa Luxemburg, *Gesammelte Werke*, vol. 4, Berlin: Dietz Verlag, 1979: 500.

57. Sender, *Autobiography of a German Rebel*: 123.

58. Ibid.: 124.

59. Ibid.: 124.

60. Carl E. Schorske, *German Social Democracy 1905–1917: The Development of the Great Schism*, Cambridge, MA: Harvard University Press, 1955: 323.

61. Theodor Plivier, *The Kaiser Goes: The Generals Remain*, in Harlan R. Crippen (ed.), *Germany: A Self-Portrait*, London: Oxford University Press, 1944: 125–6.

62. John W. Wheeler-Bennett, *The Nemesis of Power: The German Army in Politics, 1918–1945*, London: Macmillan Co., 1953: 28.

63. Scheidemann, *Memorien eines Sozialdemokraten*: 281.

64. Nigel Jones, *The Birth of the Nazis: How the Freikorps Blazed a Trail for Hitler*, London: Robinson, 2004: 41.

65. Erwin Könnemann, "Der Truppenmarsch am 10. Dezember in Berlin, Neue Dokumente zur November-Revolution," *Zeitschrift für Geschechtswissenschaft*, 3(5), 1955: 687–704.

66. Friedrich Stampfer, *Die ersten 14 Jahre der Deutschen Republik*, Offenbach a.M.: Bollwerk-Verllag K. Drott, 1947: 85.
67. Sebastian Haffner, *Failure of a Revolution: Germany 1918/19*, London: Andre Deutsch, 1973: 124.
68. Richard Müller, *Der Bürgerkrieg in Deutschland*, Berlin: Phoebus-Verlag, 1925: 9.
69. *Die Rote Fahne*, 25 December 25, 1918: 1.
70. Müller, *Der Bürgerkrieg in Deutschland*: 20–24.
71. Robert Waite comments on this error of judgement: "and it proved to be a fatal one—was in continuing to rely on the Army even after it proved faithless and in failing to try to build an army sympathetic to the Republic until it was much too late." Robert Waite, *Vanguard of Nazism*, Cambridge, MA: Harvard University Press, 1952: 6.

6. *Provocation, Revolt and Repression*

1. N. P. Howard, "The social and political consequences of the Allied food blockade of Germany, 1918–1919," *German History*, 11(2), April 1993: 161–88.
2. Toni Sender, *The Autobiography of a German Rebel*, New York: Vanguard Press, 1939: 119.
3. Howard, "The social and political consequences of the Allied food blockade of Germany, 1918–1919": 161.
4. Ibid.: 186.
5. Ibid.: 182.
6. Richard Bessel, "State and society in Germany in the aftermath of the First World War," in W. R. Lee and Eve Rosenhaft (eds.), *State, Social Policy and Social Change in Germany, 1880–1994*, Oxford: Berg, 1990: 219.
7. Ottokar Luban, "The role of the Spartacist Group after 9 November 1918 and the formation of the KPD," in Ralf Hoffrogge and Norman LaPorte, *Weimar Communism as*

Mass Movement, 1918–1933, London: Lawrence & Wishart, 2017.

8. His-Huey Liang, *The Berlin Police Force in the Weimar Republic*, Berkeley, CA: University of California Press, 1970: 33–40.

9. Richard Müller, *Der Bürgerkrieg in Deutschland*, Berlin: Phoebus-Verlag, 1925: 26–9.

10. *Die Rote Fahne*, January 5, 1919: 1.

11. See Ottokar Luban, "Rosa at a loss: The KPD leadership and the Berlin uprising of January 1919: Legend and reality," *Revolutionary History*, 8(4), 2004: 19–45.

12. Ibid.: 24.

13. Eric Waldman, *The Sparacist Uprising of 1919 and the Crisis of the German Socialist Movement: A Study of the Relation of Political Theory and Party Practice*, Milwaukee, WI: Marquette University Press, 1958: 177–8.

14. Luban, "Rosa at a loss": 25.

15. This saying is attributed to Marxist Historian Franz Mehring but was repeated by many people.

16. Luban, "Rosa at a loss": 32–40.

17. Paul Frölich, *Rosa Luxemburg: Ideas in Action*, London: Pluto Press, 1972: 288–9.

18. Luban, "Rosa at a loss": 33.

19. Ibid.: 33–5.

20. Mark Jones, *Founding Weimar: Violence and the German Revolution of 1918–1919*, Cambridge: Cambridge University Press, 2016: 225.

21. Nigel Jones, *The Birth of the Nazis: How the Freikorps Blazed a Trail for Hitler*, London: Robinson, 2004: 60–69.

22. Details of the murders are in ibid.: 74–8.

23. Bertolt Brecht, *Poems, 1913–1956*, London: Methuen, 1987: 176.

24. Jones, *Founding Weimar*: 239.

25. Ibid.: 239.

26. Ibid.: 240.

27. Pierre Broué, *The German Revolution, 1917–1923*, Chicago, IL: Haymarket Books, 2006: 971.

28. Victor Klemperer, *Munich 1919: Diary of a Revolution*, Cambridge: Polity Press, 2017: 53–7.

29. An interesting if hardly objective biography is that of his widow: Rosa Leviné-Meyer, *Leviné: The Life of a Revolutionary*, Hampshire: Saxon House, 1973.

30. Sender, *Autobiography of a German Rebel*: 146.

31. Broué, *The German Revolution, 1917–1923*: 963.

32. Charles B. Burdick and Ralph Lutz (eds.), *The Political Institutions of the German Revolution, 1918–1919*, New York: Frederick A. Praeger Publishers, 1966: 238.

33. Karl E. Meyer, *Karl Liebknecht: Man Without a Country*, Washington, DC: Public Affairs Press, 1957: 170.

34. S. Miles Bouton, *And the Kaiser Abdicates: The German Revolution, 1918–1919*, New Haven, CT: Yale University Press, 1920: 23.

35. Dieter Baudis and Hermann Roth, "Berliner Opfer der Novemberrevolution 1918–1919: eine Analyse ihre sozialen Struktur," *Jahrbuch für wirtschaftengescichte und praktische Tierzucht*, 2, 1968: 73–149.

36. Ibid.: 126–49.

37. Ibid.: 99–101.

38. Jones, *Founding Weimar*: 245–6; John Riddell, *The German Revolution and the Debate on Soviet Power*, New York: Pathfinder Press, 1986: 271–2.

39. Nadine Rossol, "Incapable of securing order? The Prussian police and the German Revolution 1918/19" in Klaus Weinhauer, Anthony McElligott and Kirsten Heinsohn (eds.), *Germany 1916–23: A Revolution in Context*, Bielefeld: Transcript Verlag, 2015: 75.

40. Oskar Hippe, *And Red is the Colour of Our Flag: Memoirs of Sixty Years in the Workers' Movement*, Richmond: Index Books, 1990: ch. 4.

41. Ernst Toller, *I was a German: The Autobiography of a Revolutionary*, New York: Paragon House, 1991: 159.
42. Ibid.: 161.
43. Ibid.: 162.
44. Ibid.: 162–3.
45. Ibid.: 164.
46. Leviné's widow later attempted a justification but it remains unconvincing. See Leviné-Meyer, *Leviné*: 120–23.
47. Allen Mitchell, *Revolution in Bavaria 1918–1919: The Eisner Regime and the Soviet Republic*, Princeton, NJ: Princeton University Press, 1965: 322–31.
48. Jones, *Founding Weimar*: 287.
49. Robert Gerwarth, "The Central European counter-revolution: Paramilitary violence in Germany, Austria and Hungary after the Great War," *Past & Present*, 200, August 2008: 203.
50. Jones, *Founding Weimar*: 312.
51. Georg Lukacs, *Lenin: A Study on the Unity of His Thought*, Cambridge, MA: MIT Press, 1971: 65.
52. Ben Fowkes, *The German Left and the Weimar Republic: A Selection of Documents*, Chicago, IL: Haymarket Books, 2015: 25.
53. Ibid.: 31.
54. Sender, *Autobiography of a German Rebel*: 142.
55. Feldman, "The social and economic policies of German big business, 1918–1929": 48.
56. Fowkes, *The German Left and the Weimar Republic*: 33.
57. Albert T. Lauterbach, "Economic demobilization in a conquered country: Germany 1919–1923," *The Journal of Politics*, 6(1), February 1944: 35.
58. Herbert Marcuse, *Five Lectures*, Boston, MA: Beacon Press, 1970: 201.
59. Heinz Brandt, *The Search for a Third Way*, Garden City, NY: Doubleday & Co., 1970: 41–4.

60. Heinrich Böll, *Group Portrait with Lady*, New York: Avon Books, 1974: 22.

61. Michael Jones, "'Can one go along with this?' German diplomats and the changes of 1918–19 and 1933–34," *Journal of Contemporary History*, 47(2), April 2012: 266.

62. William Mulligan, "Civil–military relations in the early Weimar Republic," *The Historical Journal*, 45(4), December 2002: 823.

63. Ibid.: 841.

64. Evelyn Anderson, *Hammer or Anvil: The Story of the German Working-Class Movement*, London: Victor Gollancz, 1945: 61.

7.   Women in the War and the Revolution

1. Kathleen Canning, "Gender and the imaginary of revolution in Germany," in Klaus Weinhauer, Anthony McElligott and Kirsten Heinsohn (eds.), *Germany 1916–23: A Revolution in Context*, Bielefeld: Transcript Verlag, 2015: 109.

2. Georg Adler, Peter Hudis and Annelies Laschitza (eds.), *The Letters of Rosa Luxemburg*, London: Verso, 2011: 481.

3. Ibid.: 483.

4. Mark Jones, *Founding Weimar: Violence and the German Revolution of 1918–1919*, Cambridge: Cambridge University Press, 2016: 157.

5. Helen Boak, *Women in the Weimar Republic*, Manchester: Manchester University Press, 2013: 38.

6. Jones, *Founding Weimar*: 157.

7. Richard Bessel, *Germany after the First World War*, Oxford: Clarendon Press, 2002: 239.

8. Ute Daniel, *The War Within: German Working Class Women in the First World War*, New York: Berg, 1997: 249.

9. US Department of Commerce and Labor, Bureau of Statistics, *Industrial Education and Industrial Conditions in*

Germany, Washington, DC: Government Printing Office, 1905: 198.

10. Kathleen Canning, *Languages of Labor and Gender: Female Factory Work in Germany, 1850–1914*, Ithaca, NY: Cornell University Press, 1996: 178.

11. Ibid.: 182.

12. Nancy Reagin, "The imaginary *Hausfrau*: National identity, domesticity, and colonialism in Imperial Germany," *The Journal of Modern History*, 73(1), March 2001: 64.

13. Ibid.: 66.

14. Seth Koven and Sonya Michel, "Womanly duties: Materialist politics and the origins of welfare states in France, Germany, Great Britain and the United States, 1880–1920," *The American Historical Review*, 95(4), October 1990: 1077.

15. "Infant welfare in Germany during the War," *Public Health Reports (1896–1970)*, 34(7), February 14, 1919: 279.

16. Kathleen Canning, *Gender History in Practice: Historical Perspectives on Bodies, Class and Citizenship*, Ithaca, NY: Cornell University Press: 21–8.

17. R. P. Neuman, "Working class birth control in Wilhelmine Germany," *Comparative Studies in Society and History*, 20(3), July 1978: 417.

18. Ibid.: 418.

19. Jo Jones, William Mosher and Kimberly Daniels, "Current contraceptive use in the United States, 2006–2010, and changes in patterns of use since 1995," *National Health Statistics Reports*, 60, October 18, 2012, retrieved on September 20, 2017 from www.cdc.gov/nchs/data/nhsr/nhsr060.pdf.

20. Jeffrey S. Richter, "Infanticide, child abandonment and abortion in Imperial Germany," *The Journal of Interdisciplinary History*, 28(4), Spring 1998: 514.

21. Ibid.: 526.

22. Richard J. Evans, "Prostitution, state and society in Imperial Germany," *Past & Present*, 70, February 1976: 116–17.

23. August Bebel, *Woman and Socialism*, New York: Socialist Literature Company, 1910: 195.
24. Werner Thönnessen, *The Emancipation of Women: The Rise and Decline of the Women's Movement in German Social Democracy, 1863–1933*, London: Pluto Press, 1973: 51.
25. Evans: 129.
26. Kathleen Canning, "Gender and the politics of class formation: Rethinking German labor history," *The American Historical Review*, 87(3), June 1992: 757.
27. Thönnessen, *The Emancipation of Women*: 76.
28. Bebel's book has been called "the bible of socialist women." Koven and Michel, "Womanly duties": 1091.
29. Lise Vogel, *Marxism and the Oppression of Women: Toward a Unitary Theory*, Chicago, IL: Haymarket Books, 2013: 100.
30. Karen Honeycutt, "Socialism and feminism in Imperial Germany," *Signs*, 5(1), Autumn 1979: 33.
31. Karl Marx and Friedrich Engels, *Collected Works*, vol. 26, London: Lawrence & Wishart, 2010: 262. For a useful discussion of *Origin of the Family, Private Property and the State*, see Joesette Trat, "Engels and the emancipation of women," *Science & Society*, 62(1), Spring 1998: 88–105.
32. Karen Honeycutt, "Clara Zetkin: A socialist approach to the problem of women's oppression," in Jane Slaughter and Robert Kern (eds.), *European Women on the Left: Socialism, Feminism and the Problems Faced by Political Women, 1880 to the Present*, London: Greenwood Press, 1981: 41.
33. Thönnessen, *The Emancipation of Women*: 77.
34. Belinda J. Davis, *Home Fires Burning: Food, Politics and Everyday Life in World War I Berlin*, Chapel Hill, NC: University of North Carolina Press, 2000: 53.
35. Clara Zetkin, *Selected Writings*, ed. Philip S. Foner, Chicago, IL: Haymarket Books, 2015: 130–32.
36. Susan Zimmermann, "Clara Zetkin goes international: The Socialist Women's International and unequal European and global order, 1901–1917," in Marilyn J. Boxer and John S.

Partington (eds.), *Clara Zetkin: National and International Context*, London: Socialist History Society, 2013: 69.

37. Toni Sender, *The Autobiography of a German Rebel*, New York: Vanguard Press, 1939: 74.

38. Carl E. Schorske, *German Social Democracy 1905–1917: The Development of the Great Schism*, Cambridge, MA: Harvard University Press, 1955: 212.

39. Thönnessen, *The Emancipation of Women*: 80.

40. Ibid.: 87.

41. Daniel, *The War Within*: 250.

42. Davis, *Home Fires Burning*: 225.

43. Hermann Duncker and Käte Duncker, *Ein Tagebuch in Briefen (1894–1953)*, Berlin: Dietz Verlag, 2016: 2465–6.

44. Sender, *Autobiography of a German Rebel*: 83.

45. Canning, "Gender and the politics of class formation": 764.

46. Pierre Broué, *The German Revolution, 1917–1923*, Chicago, IL: Haymarket Books, 2006: 96.

47. Ralf Hoffrogge, *Working Class Politics in the German Revolution: Richard Müller, the Revolutionary Shop Stewards and the Origins of the Council Movement*, Chicago, IL: Haymarket Books, 2015: 51.

48. Davis, *Home Fires Burning*: 202.

49. Canning, "Gender and the imaginary of revolution in Germany": 108.

50. Ibid.

51. Ibid.: 119.

52. Richard J. Evans, "German social democracy and women's suffrage, 1891–1918," *Journal of Contemporary History*, 15(3), July 1980: 534.

53. Thönnessen, *The Emancipation of Women*: 67.

54. Evans, "German social democracy and women's suffrage, 1891–1918": 540.

55. Ibid.: 542.

56. Kathleen Canning, "Claiming citizenship: Suffrage and subjectivity in Germany after the First World War," in Kathleen

Canning, Kerstin Barndt and Kristin McGuire (eds.), *Weimar Publics/Weimar Subjects: Rethinking the Political Culture of Germany in the 1920s*, New York: Berghahn Books, 2010: 127.

57. Evans, "German social democracy and women's suffrage, 1891–1918": 552.
58. Ibid.: 555.
59. Thönnessen, *The Emancipation of Women*: 86.
60. Canning, "Gender and the imaginary of revolution in Germany": 119.
61. Jones, *Founding Weimar*: 24.
62. Robert Gerwarth, "The Central European counter-revolution: Paramilitary violence in Germany, Austria and Hungary after the Great War," *Past & Present*, 200, August 2008: 203.
63. Jones, *Founding Weimar*: 25.
64. Ute L. Tellini, "Max Beckmann's 'tribute' to Rosa Luxemburg," *Woman's Art Journal*, 18(2), Autumn 1997–Winter 1998: 22.
65. Ibid.: 23.
66. Jones, *Founding Weimar*: 216.
67. Ibid.: 217.
68. Ibid.: 218ff.
69. Sender, *Autobiography of a German Rebel*: 153.
70. Duncker and Duncker, *Ein Tagebuch in Briefen (1894–1953)*: 3106.

8. Death Agony of the Revolution

1. Nigel Jones, *The Birth of the Nazis: How the Freikorps Blazed a Trail for Hitler*, London: Robinson, 2004: 171.
2. Toni Sender, *The Autobiography of a German Rebel*, New York: Vanguard Press, 1939: 151.
3. Jones, *The Birth of the Nazis*: 180.

4. "Joint call by German trade unions for a general strike against Kapp Putsch, 13 March 1920," in Ben Fowkes, *The German Left and the Weimar Republic: A Selection of Documents*, Chicago, IL: Haymarket Books, 2015: 113–14.

5. Adam Roberts, "Civil resistance to military coups," *Journal of Peace Research*, 12(1), 1975: 22.

6. Jones, *The Birth of the Nazis*: 172.

7. Pierre Broué, *The German Revolution, 1917–1923*, Chicago, IL: Haymarket Books, 2006: 355.

8. Sender, *Autobiography of a German Rebel*: 152.

9. Broué, *The German Revolution, 1917–1923*: 356.

10. Ibid.: 359.

11. Roberts, "Civil resistance to military coups": 23.

12. Broué, *The German Revolution, 1917–1923*: 360.

13. Sender, *Autobiography of a German Rebel*: 157.

14. Jones, *The Birth of the Nazis*: 188.

15. Broué, *The German Revolution, 1917–1923*: 364.

16. Sender, *Autobiography of a German Rebel*: 147–8.

17. Arthur Rosenberg, *A History of the German Republic*, London: Methuen & Co., 1936: 333–5.

18. Jones, *The Birth of the Nazis*: 189.

19. Roberts, "Civil resistance to military coups": 22.

20. Leon Trotsky, *History of the Russian Revolution*, Chicago, IL: Haymarket Books, 2017: 899.

21. Robert F. Wheeler, "German Labor and the Comintern: A problem of generations?," *Journal of Social History*, 7(3), March 1974: 304–21.

22. Debs spent many years in Federal Prison for speaking against the US involvement in World War I. He ran for President in 1920, from his Atlanta prison cell, and again received almost a million votes.

23. William A. Pelz (ed.), *The Eugene V. Debs Reader: Socialism and the Class Struggle*, London: Merlin Press, 2014: 211.

24. Evelyn Anderson, *Hammer or Anvil: The Story of the German Working-Class Movement*, London: Victor Gollancz, 1945: 61: 47.
25. Maximillian, Prince of Baden, *The Memoirs of Prince Max of Baden*, vol. II, New York: Charles Scribner's Sons, 1928: 196.
26. Mark Jones, *Founding Weimar: Violence and the German Revolution of 1918–1919*, Cambridge: Cambridge University Press, 2016: 32–43.
27. Typical is Weitz, *Weimar Germany: Promise and Tragedy*: 100, 111–12.
28. Michael Geyer, "Insurrectionary warfare: The German debate about a *levée en masse* in October 1918," *The Journal of Modern History*, 73(3), September 2001: 482–3.
29. Weitz, *Weimar Germany: Promise and Tragedy*: 13.
30. Maximillian, Prince of Baden, *The Memoirs of Prince Max of Baden*, vol. II: 200.
31. Kathleen Canning, "Feminist history after the linguistic turn: Historicizing discourse and experience," *Signs*, 19(2), Winter 1994: 384–5.
32. Werner Thönnessen, *The Emancipation of Women: The Rise and Decline of the Women's Movement in German Social Democracy, 1863–1933*, London: Pluto Press, 1973: 105.
33. Ibid.: 106.
34. Some argue that only large landowners and war industries like Krupp prospered during the war. See Joerg Baten and Rainer Schulz, "Making profits in wartime: Corporate profits, inequality, and GDP in Germany during the First World War," *The Economic History Review*, new series, 58(1), February 2005: 34–56.
35. Richard Bessel, *Germany after the First World War*, Oxford: Clarendon Press, 2002: 100–101.
36. Weitz, *Weimar Germany: Promise and Tragedy*: 21.
37. Bessel, *Germany after the First World War*: 248.
38. Ibid.: 236–7.

39. Christopher Dillon, "'We'll meet again in Dachau': The early Dachau SS and the narrative of Civil War," *Journal of Contemporary History*, 45(3), July 2010: 541.
40. Karl Liebknecht, "Despite it all!," in Gabriel Kuhn (ed.), *All Power to the Councils: A Documentary History of the German Revolution of 1918–1919*, Oakland, CA: PM Press, 2012: 124.
41. Jones, "The crowd in the German November Revolution": 56.
42. Matthew Richardson, *The Hunger War: Food, Rations and Rationing, 1914–1918*, Barnsby: Pen & Sword Books, 2015: 163.
43. Quoted in John Riddell, *The German Revolution and the Debate on Soviet Power*, New York: Pathfinder Press, 1986: 213.
44. Paul Frölich, quoted in Riddell, *The German Revolution and the Debate on Soviet Power*: 227.
45. Frölich, ibid.: 228.
46. Bessel, *Germany after the First World War*: 190.
47. Fowkes, *The German Left and the Weimar Republic*: 35.
48. Ibid.: 36.
49. Bessel, *Germany after the First World War*: 135.
50. Ibid.: 143.
51. Michael Hirsch, "Contra Bronner on Luxemburg and working-class revolution," in Jason Schulman (ed.), *Rosa Luxemburg: Her Life and Legacy*, New York: Palgrave Macmillan, 2013: 176.

Conclusion

1. Helen Boak, "'What they can do in Russia, so can we': The impact of the Russian Revolutions of 1917 in Germany," in David Morgan (ed.), *1917: The Russian Revolution, Reactions and Impact*, London: Socialist History Society, 2017: 34.

2. V. I. Lenin, *Left-Wing Communism: An Infantile Disorder*, New York: International Publishers, 1940: 55.

3. Robert Gerwarth, "The Central European Counter-Revolution: Paramilitary violence in Germany, Austria and Hungary after the Great War," *Past & Present*, 200, August 2008: 203.

4. Tariq Ali, *The Extreme Centre: A Warning*, London: Verso, 2015.

5. Mark Jones, *Founding Weimar: Violence and the German Revolution of 1918–1919*, Cambridge: Cambridge University Press, 2016: 5.

6. Toni Sender, *The Autobiography of a German Rebel*, New York: Vanguard Press, 1939: 165.

7. One of the best written from this political viewpoint is Chris Harman, *The Lost Revolution: Germany 1918–1923*, London: Bookmarks, 1997.

8. Carl E. Schorske, *German Social Democracy 1905–1917: The Development of the Great Schism*, Cambridge, MA: Harvard University Press, 1955: 124.

9. Sender, *Autobiography of a German Rebel*: 272.

10. Rosa Luxemburg, *Revolutionary Socialist Organization*, New York: Integer Press, 1934: 19–20.

Index

abortion 106–7
Abrams, Lynn 20
Addams, Jane 42
alcohol 11–12
Algerian soldiers 36
All Quiet on the Western Front
  (Remarque) 49
Anderson, Evelyn 100–1
anti-Semitism *xvii–xviii*, 94
Arensee, Martha 116
army
  Army High Command 81–2,
    119–22, 127, 135
  drafting of strikers into 58, 60,
    113
  Ebert-Groener pact 81–2
  fraternization 34–8
  soldiers' attitude to war 30–1,
    45, 46–7, 49
Artelt, Karl 63
At the Loom of Time: A Social-
  political Novel (Otto-Walster)
  21
Austro-Hungarian Empire 59

barmaids 5
Bavarian Socialist Republic 96–7
Bebel, August 15, 17, 22, 107, 108
Beckmann, Max 117
Bergg, Franz 6–7
Bernstein, Eduard 17, 58, 76
birth control 106
birth rate 49

Bismarck, Otto von *viii*, 1–2,
  15–16, 27
black markets 39, 41
Blücher, Princess Evelyn 53, 77
Böhm, Gustav 77–8
Böll, Heinrich 99–100
Bolsheviks 56, 136 *see also* Russian
  Revolution
Brandt, Heinz 99
Braun, Lily 32
bread riots 32–3, 41
Brecht, Bertolt 93
Bremen Soviet Republic 95

Canning, Kathleen 78
capitalists
  feudal lords, struggle with 2
  military and *x*
  Nazis and 137
  during November revolution
    57, 69
  postwar 128–9, 133
  SPD and 99
Carr, E.H. *xvi*
child mortality 50
Christmas truce 35–7
Churchill, Winston *xvii–xviii*
class consciousness/identity 9,
  20–1
collective bargaining 133
communists *see* KPD
conferences 41–2, 110–11
confirmation bias *xvii*